Retirement on a Shoestring

Ideas in Support of a Fearless, Creative Final Chapter

Candy Carlberg

ISBN: 978-1-962624-71-8

Dedication

This book is dedicated to Ford, who taught me to open my heart to the next adventure.

Acknowledgment

I wish to acknowledge Elizabeth Gilbert, particularly her book *Big Magic*, for inspiration. Her ability to paint a picture of *"creative living beyond fear"* has been a critical support during my process of envisioning a retirement plan that makes my heart soar.

Table Of Contents

About the Author

This book is not written from the perspective of an authority, financial or otherwise, on retirement. It is instead a personal account of my journey into my 60s and now 70s, having missed the memo somehow in my early career about the importance of planning for this chapter of life.

A key ingredient for staying on the side of gratitude and positivity throughout this process is 1) that I can hold in my heart both a powerful appreciation for my work, in that it keeps me challenged emotionally and mentally, as well as in daily teamwork with a diverse group of younger colleagues, and 2) my deep trust that we are all exactly where we are meant to be; where our choices have brought us, therefore the perspective of being a victim has no place in this paradigm.

My husband of 23 years during the '60s, '70s, and well into the '80s was one of those rare beings who immersed himself in a life of joy and curiosity. In our early life together, we lived on the edge of the beaches of Southern California, basking in the sun by day and walking miles of the magical beach by night. We owned a small health foods store in Colorado that became a hub for a community of uniquely interesting people. We traveled to Germany to live and work on a biodynamic farm with other young change-makers from all over Europe. These were experiences that shifted the very foundation of my soul.

I later found myself suited, maybe gifted, in the art of teaching children and adolescents who struggle with emotional and cognitive challenges. These students taught me to choose my battles and not sweat the small stuff.

All of these rich aspects of my life now accompany me in exploring how I want to design the years to come. I am grateful every day for my ability to surrender to this process and find joy in the seeking.

As Jane Fonda says in her book Prime Time, *"If we can learn to assign new meanings to stressful situations, we can actually avoid the biochemical and hormonal reactions that cause damage to our systems, especially with age."*

This is the approach to living I hope to inspire those having to design a retirement that affords them the right balance of solitude, joyful connection, financial freedom, and grace they deserve during the final chapter of life.

Preface

Welcome, dear friends, to a tale untold,
Of fearless hearts and dreams of gold,
Retirement's door swings open wide,
Adventure calls, let's take the ride!
With laughter and mischief, we'll begin,
Embracing age, no time for chagrin,
I faced the skeptics, their doubtful gaze,
But I chose to wander uncharted ways.
In "downhill" claims, I found no truth,
For in this chapter, I found my youth,
With curiosity, my heart did swell,
A creative approach, I'd boldly sell.
A rebel spirit, I took the lead,
A "go with the flow" life, yes indeed,
But alas, retirement planning fell shy,
My golden years needed wings to fly.
Alternative streams I sought to explore,
From ADUs to tutoring galore,
And oh, the tales that I can tell,
Of trying it all, how time did swell!

Retirement on a Shoestring

I played the notary, a star with a seal,
And furnished rooms, oh, what a deal,
Yet, in this quest, my heart did yearn,
For the perfect fit, where passions burn.
With gratitude, I embraced my role,
An inspiring teacher, heart and soul,
But this adventure held even more,
From copywriting gigs to a health coach's lore.
Oh, the wonders of a growth mindset,
With meditation, dreams I met,
In fitness, I danced with pure delight,
Seeking inspiration, day and night.
Let's shatter the myth of age's cage,
Our spirit, unbound, on every stage,
Retirement's not a time to fade,
But to savor life's grand escapade.
So, raise a cheer, and let's begin,
The magic of retirement, let it all sink in.
With courage and joy, let's face the unknown,
With open hearts, let dreams be sown,
This is the story we all can weave,
A tale of love, the will to believe.
So, grab your chair, and let's unfold,

A tale of silver and of gold,

In *"Retirement on a Shoestring,"* we find,

A journey of hearts, forever entwined.

With love and excitement, we'll journey ahead,

To a fearless retirement where dreams are spread,

This is our moment; let's seize the day,

In the art of aging, we'll find our way.

Chapter 1: Rediscovery

"Count your age by friends, not years. Count your life by smiles, not tears."

-John Lennon

As pretty as that sentiment is, the truth of aging is that not many of us plan on doing so, particularly in a culture that places such high value on youth. Retirement is a time when you are supposed to be reaping the fruits of your labor throughout your life.

For many, this ideal is undermined by loss of health, mobility, or vitality. In my case, this ideal is sabotaged by a lack of adequate financial resources. For various reasons, this can be said for many in my age group, if not the majority. So many live from paycheck to paycheck with just enough income to get by, so saving a portion of those earnings is not possible.

Many have various retirement plans available through their employer that fall far short of adequate when retirement age arrives. My years of working in the non-profit sector did not provide a plan with any employer contributions, and I was never frugal or wise enough to create an alternative plan on my own.

For many, the idea of retirement may inspire dread that is on par with death. This is especially true of professionals who have derived their sense of self-worth from their work, with few other interests to balance their lives.

The fear of growing old or irrelevant, loss of autonomy, chronic illnesses, and other worries are quite common as we age and may trigger avoidant behaviors where we procrastinate our way through life without a plan until we are face-to-face with the question of how we will support ourselves during the final years of life.

This book is a shared exploration of ideas for those retired, swiftly approaching retirement age, or even the young *(it is better to plan now than worry later)* so that you can genuinely enjoy your Golden Years as they are meant to be enjoyed—no matter what that looks like for you.

My name is Candy Carlberg, and I am writing this book because I've had to negotiate a path into *"retirement"* at a very late date.

Now, in my seventies, I look back and realize that, in my sixties, I unfortunately missed a crucial lesson in my early career: the importance of planning ahead for this stage of life. This book is my account of my journey through this experience to hopefully serve as inspiration for those who might find themselves in a similar situation as I am.

I worked in special education for nearly three decades and counting. I am by far the oldest person on my school campus and am currently on a journey to create a sustainable retirement plan for myself *(a bit late, I know, but that is the whole point of this book, is it not?).*

I have been blessed to be able to work two days per week this school year, which has provided me with time to research other avenues of growth and other sources of income. During this period, it has been vital to me to actively increase the soulful quality of my life in a way that allows me to perceive my current situation as an opportunity to be grateful.

The first piece of advice that I can give anyone in a similar position is to change their view of retirement and aging!

In the "*olden days*" (ha-ha!), you could get away with having one job and retiring to a more *"chill"* life, but with the current state of the economy and the world, that has become more of a dream than a reality for many.

While I do believe the universe will provide, this trust must be balanced with inner work so that the heart is open to guidance. Once you begin to research alternative means of income and lifestyle, intuition keeps you aligned with your deeper purpose and intention. Inspiration is a critical ingredient in the process of reinventing your retirement life.

In her book, "*Big Magic*," author Elizabeth Gilbert describes this quality as "creative living beyond fear." The following passage is a favorite of mine.

"And you have treasures hidden within you —extraordinary treasures— and so do I, and so does everyone around us. And bringing those treasures to light takes work and faith and focus and courage and hours of devotion, and the clock is ticking, and the world is spinning, and we simply do not have time anymore to think so small."

We need to excavate said treasures, take more chances on ourselves, and harness our creativity to the best of our ability.

I am not recommending you work so hard and *"grind"* until you are comfortable; that is a false belief, and we are well past those days *(thank God!)*.

Now is the time to work smart, not hard.

Planning conscientious and incremental changes is much better and much more sustainable than expecting to transform your life in one fell swoop.

The universe has always come through for me, and I ask you to do your due diligence and leave the rest to God, to providence, or to the universe, whatever you wish. However, the due diligence part is up to you. It's a divine partnership, if you will, and the more joy you can bring to the process, the more inspired retired life you will create. Fear is the obstacle to remaining joyful and inspired throughout this process.

There was no definitive guide out there that could have helped me through this time in my life, so I decided to write one myself in the form of this personal account to share in hopes that it would open the door for someone else to celebrate a challenge that our culture wants to frame as a "*failure*" or "*crisis*."

I hope this account of my process of creative retirement on a shoestring helps someone to steer clear of a fear-based perspective on planning their retirement, whatever age you decide to do it!

I am not a financial planner, a motivational guru, or a medical practitioner- I am writing this book as a documentation of my journey toward retirement.

So, dear reader, what can you expect further in this book?

Well, I will go over my own "*misadventures*" as a non-planner and the richness of those experiences that provide the tapestry of my retired life.

I will discuss my research regarding alternative income streams (passive income especially) and, finally, some self-care tools that have supported me in becoming my best self as I continue to build a sustainable and deeply satisfying retirement.

Happy reading, happy planning, and happy retirement!

Chapter 2:
Unplanned Retirement Plans

"The real voyage of discovery consists not in seeking new landscapes, but in having new eyes."

—Marcel Proust

If, like myself and so many others of a certain age, you find yourself insufficiently prepared for retirement, or as Jane Fonda describes it, "the final act," move as quickly as possible through and past all self-deprecatory regrets.

Stay positive!

Cultivate gratitude and open your heart to all possibilities for a new vision. If this is new to you, it's an excellent time to research ideas like vision boards, practicing positive affirmations, etc.

We will dive into this in more depth in a later chapter, but it's essential to set the stage now with a mindset of anticipation and trust that picking up this book is a stepping stone to a creative future.

Before moving into a discussion of some of the nuts-and-bolts ideas for alternative income streams that I have explored, I would like to turn back the clock to an earlier transformative period in my life, which literally provided me with *"new eyes"* at a critical threshold as I was stepping into adulthood.

It was in the 1960s when I met my husband in college in Southern California, in the milieu of nationwide social and political activism. My generation then congregated and started to question the social spheres and practices they grew up with. They strived to rethink general society and its constraints on the average person. This cultural shift quite literally shook the foundations of society as we knew it. It was a cultural and creative renaissance when the social norms of consumerism and conformity had become the essence of the *"American dream."*

Amid this cultural upheaval, we both decided not to return to school that fall and instead loaded my husband's car to the gills and headed for the Rocky Mountains and the State of Colorado—his hometown state. His family had travel experience both nationally and internationally, but I had rarely traveled out of my small California town, where not only I but my mother and grandmother had grown up. So, this was a great adventure for me, and I was excited to see what life had in store for us!

After a breathtaking drive through the mountains, we stayed at his friend's place for a while and rented out a house in Denver. One month later, it was apparent that we could not make rent. So, I sewed several peasant shirts out of muslin fabric that we embroidered with colorful designs. We then hung them around on a tree on the campus at the University of Denver. We met many intriguing people there throughout the day, had a wonderful time, and made enough money to cover the rent for that month.

We ultimately ended up in Greeley, Colorado, where a local health food store was essentially gifted to us. Our son's birth coincided with establishing a close-knit community centered around the health food store and its lively bulletin board. During this time, we also developed an interest in organic farming and later pursued it all the way to Germany to work on a biodynamic farm for a year.

These were the years of my life when I adopted my *go-with-the-flow* approach and learned to trust the process without being threatened by the fear of the unknown.

The origin of the flow approach dates back to the Roman Emperor Marcus Aurelius. He apparently encouraged people not to waste energy and fight against society but rather to accept things as they are and just go along with them.

In his case, this concept aimed to encourage a compliant society. Still, the saying has morphed to mean one should tune in to a higher order and live in harmony with the natural flow of life. Going with the flow also means that no matter how much structure we try to create in our lives, there will always be things we cannot control.

The struggle for control originates from a fear-based mindset. Fear is always about contraction. This book is about the opposite: expansion. It requires an open heart and mind to experience our "retirement" years from a place of creativity and exploration rather than fear and contraction. It also requires a good measure of courage.

This said, there is undoubtedly a place for balance between rigid control and structured planning and surrendering to what our life's larger purpose has in store for us! I found out ignorance isn't bliss when planning and providing for my retirement years.

I did not make smart choices when it came to money. I also must say, however, that the carefree attitude of "the universe will take care of me" that led me to be negligent about structuring a solid retirement plan years ago is the same saving grace quality that allows me to rarely feel fearful at 73 because, in all honesty, the universe has always come through.

But we must accept that life is unpredictable and that sometimes you must just roll with the punches. However, this doesn't mean you should be unprepared. In fact, planning ahead and being proactive is the best way to ensure that you have a secure financial future.

Procrastination is one of the biggest mistakes people make regarding retirement planning. We often think we have plenty of time, but the years can fly by quickly; before we know it, we're already in our 60s or 70s. That's why it's imperative to start planning for retirement as early as possible, even if it's just a small amount of money each month. The earlier you start, the more time your money has to grow, and the more likely you are to achieve your goals.

It's also important to consider the impact of inflation when planning for retirement. As prices rise over time, the money you'll need to live on will increase. This means you'll need to save more now than you would have if you'd started earlier. The good news is that there are many ways to counteract the effects of inflation, such as investing in stocks and bonds, which can help your money grow over time.

It's a common misconception that relying solely on social security will be enough to provide for ourselves in our golden years.

Unfortunately, this couldn't be further from the truth. As we've seen, many of our peers continue working well into their old age, whether as Walmart greeters or fast food servers, simply because they haven't saved enough for their retirement. This can be a harsh reality for many, but it's significant to understand why relying solely on social security is inadequate and what we can do to avoid the same fate.

Firstly, let's look at the current state of social security. It's no secret that the Social Security Trust Fund is facing serious financial challenges. The number of retirees drawing benefits is growing, while the number of workers contributing to the fund is shrinking.

This puts a tremendous strain on the system, and many experts believe that the trust fund will be depleted by 2035. If nothing changes, social security benefits will need to be reduced, leaving retirees with even less money to support themselves.

In addition to the financial challenges facing the social security system, it's important to understand that social security was never meant to be the sole source of retirement income.

Social security benefits are designed to replace only a portion of your pre-retirement income, typically around 40%. That means that even if the trust fund remains solvent, you can still expect a significant reduction in your standard of living when you retire.

So, if relying on social security alone is inadequate, how can we ensure enough money to support ourselves in our retirement years?

The answer is simple: we need to save and invest. By doing so, we can supplement our social security benefits and ensure we have enough money to live comfortably in our golden years.

How do we do that without allowing ourselves to be overwhelmed?

In her book "*Prime Time*," Jane Fonda encourages readers to perform a life review, which involves reflecting on past events and experiences to understand our present and future better.

Through a life review, we can let go of old patterns, identify what is most important to us, and cultivate new goals and dreams to make the most of our mature years.

To begin your life review, start by reflecting on your past. Look at your career and personal life and identify the highs and lows. What worked and what didn't? What were your most significant accomplishments, and what were your biggest challenges?

Once you have a better understanding of your past, you can start to think about your future.

Identify what is most important to you and what you want to achieve in retirement.

Do you want to travel, volunteer, or spend time with family and friends? Do you have any financial goals, such as paying off debt or buying a new home?

With your goals in mind, it's time to start planning your finances. Start by creating a budget that reflects your current income and expenses. Look for areas where you can reduce spending and redirect those funds toward your retirement goals.

One aspect of retirement planning that is often overlooked is the importance of reflecting on our lives. We spend so much of our lives rushing from one thing to the next that we rarely have the opportunity to stop and reflect on where we have been and are going.

Self-reflection allows us to gain a deeper understanding of our life experiences and helps us make more informed decisions about our future.

When planning for retirement, it's essential to take the time to reflect on your life experiences. This reflection can help you identify your priorities and determine what is most important to you.

"By knowing our past, we gain insight into what we are capable of doing, and by reflecting on our future, we can plan for the life we want to live," says Fonda.

While a life review can be a deeply personal and emotional process, it's crucial to approach it with a positive and open mindset. It's not about dwelling on regrets or missed opportunities but rather about gaining insight and understanding of our past experiences to help guide our future.

As we approach our retirement years, it's easy to fall into the trap of thinking that life is winding down. But what if I told you that retirement can be the start of a new life? A life filled with creativity, joy, and purpose.

I want to share with you how to make the most of your retirement years by becoming proactive, having a spiritual and positive approach toward life, and embracing the positive aspects of aging.

First, let's talk about being proactive.

Retirement can be a time of uncertainty, mainly if you're used to working and having a routine. It's important to take charge of your retirement and find new ways to stay engaged with life. This might mean taking up a new hobby, volunteering, or even starting a new career. The key is to stay active and engaged with the world around you.

In her book "Big Magic: Creative Living Beyond Fear," Elizabeth Gilbert writes about the importance of creativity in our lives. She writes, "Creativity is a path for the brave, yes, but it is not a path for the fearless, and it's important to recognize the distinction." This is especially true in retirement. By embracing creativity, you can open new avenues for self-expression, personal growth, and joy.

One way to tap into your creativity in retirement is to take a class or workshop. You might learn a new skill or explore a new art form. Or, you might start a creative project of your own. It's never too late to write a book, start a blog, or create a piece of art. By embracing your creativity, you can find new ways to express yourself and connect with the world around you.

Let's talk about having a spiritual and positive approach to life. In retirement, it's easy to feel a sense of loss or sadness as we reflect on the past and worry about the future. But what if we shifted our focus to the present moment?

Gilbert also writes, "I believe that our planet is inhabited not only by animals and plants and bacteria and viruses but also by ideas. Ideas are a disembodied, energetic life-form. They are completely separate from us but capable of interacting with us—albeit strangely." This notion highlights the importance of connecting with the world around us, including our inner world.

One way to tap into your spiritual side in retirement is to practice mindfulness. This might mean meditation, yoga, or simply walking in nature. You can find peace, joy, and purpose every day by connecting with the present moment.

Finally, let's talk about embracing the positive aspects of aging. In our youth-obsessed culture, it's easy to view aging as unfavorable. But what if we reframed our perspective and saw aging as a positive thing?

Gilbert says, "Aging is not just decaying, you know. It's growth. It's more than the negative that you're going to die. It's the positive that you understand you're going to die and that you live a better life because of it." This idea highlights the importance of embracing the positive aspects of aging, including wisdom, experience, and a deeper appreciation for life.

One way to embrace the positive aspects of aging in retirement is to connect with others. This might mean spending time with family and friends, volunteering in your community, or joining a social group. Connecting with others allows you to share your wisdom and experience and find new ways to enjoy life.

So, I say I have a plan but stay open to possibilities. Especially if you are reading this during your younger years, then bravo! Start planning and creating a vision for yourself now. However, if you find yourself entering "the final act" with insufficient resources, don't let that hinder your quest from making these the most satisfying years yet, and find a way to reframe the situation as an opportunity.

Fear is truly your worst enemy.

Chapter 3: Exploring Alternative Income Streams

In the previous chapter, we talked about the importance of having a retirement plan that goes beyond just saving money. We also explored how your retirement lifestyle is key in determining how much money you'll need to save. Let's take it a step further and discuss alternative income streams.

You might be wondering,

"Why do I need to explore alternative income streams? I've got my retirement savings, and that should be enough."

Well, let me tell you, having a backup plan is always a good idea. You never know what might happen in life, and having multiple income streams can provide you with financial security and peace of mind.

Plus, who wouldn't want to have a little extra cash on hand to pursue their passions or indulge in some guilty pleasures?

Maybe you've always wanted to take up a new hobby or travel to your dream destination. Having alternative income streams can give you the financial freedom to do so.

As author Ernie J. Zelinski once said,

"Retirement is a time to experiment anew, to enjoy new interests, and to continue to grow intellectually."

Embrace this mindset, and don't be afraid to take risks. You might just stumble upon a new passion that generates some extra income!

Now, let's talk about the exciting world of alternative income streams.

In today's fast-paced society, it's becoming increasingly important to be financially independent and have the flexibility to work from home. That's why so many people are now looking for alternative income streams that allow them to work from the comfort of their own homes and be more independent in their work lives.

And guess what?

It's not just for young folks. Retirees can totally join in, too!

So, why should you explore alternative income streams, you might ask?

Well, there are tons of reasons.

Maybe you're looking for a way to supplement your current income or want to start your own business. Whatever your reason, it's significant to approach the process with an open mind and a willingness to explore new possibilities.

One of the biggest advantages of exploring alternative income streams is the potential for greater flexibility and independence.

Let's face it: traditional jobs often require you to be stuck in one location with a strict schedule that may not work for your other responsibilities, such as caring for children or elderly relatives. With alternative income streams, you have the freedom to work from anywhere, at any time, which can be a game-changer for many people.

But wait, there's more!

Another benefit of exploring alternative income streams is the potential for increased income. While traditional jobs may have a set salary, alternative income streams often offer the opportunity to earn more money through commissions, bonuses, or other incentives.

Also, starting a business can be a great way to build wealth over time and achieve financial independence.

Now, I won't lie to you. Exploring alternative income streams does come with its own set of challenges.

It can be challenging to know where to start, and there's often a steep learning curve involved in mastering a new skill or building a new business.

But fear not!

With determination, hard work, and a willingness to learn, anyone can succeed in alternative income streams.

The author of The Retirement Maze, Rob Pascale, says,

"Today's retirees can't just sit back and let their savings generate interest. They have to be more proactive and creative when it comes to generating income."

Well, I say it's time to take control of your financial future and embrace a creative, exploratory mindset in retirement.

You might just discover a new passion or talent along the way!

In my retirement journey, I've been exploring alternative income stream options; let me tell you, it's been quite an adventure.

Let me share a bit about the options I've explored so far.

First, we have the ADU, which stands for "alternative dwelling unit," or, as I like to call it, the granny unit.

The idea here is to build a small rental unit on my property to bring in some extra income. I did my due diligence and even toured some model ADUs. Still, after having some contractors come to my home and crunch the numbers, I realized that taking on a home equity loan wouldn't make sense. The construction timeline would likely take a year when I wouldn't have any additional income to pay off the loan. So, while I haven't ruled out this option altogether, I know that I need to secure another source of income first.

That brings me to my second option, working as a part-time remote adjunct faculty member for a university.

This job was a great find for me because I wanted to move away from being tied to an 8-hour workday, and my background in education allowed me to secure this remote job. The only downside is that universities typically use adjunct staff to keep costs low, which means that the pay is minimal and benefits aren't available.

But hey, it's a start and a great way to dip my toes into the world of alternative income streams.

As I've explored different options for alternative income streams in retirement, I've come across some interesting opportunities.

One option I tried was renting out my spare room on Furnished Finder, a website that connects renters with temporary living arrangements. It was a great way to make extra income, but my small house wasn't ideal for long-term rentals. If you have more space, though, I highly recommend looking into this option.

Another option that I found to be quite flexible is becoming a public notary. The training is inexpensive, and the fees for each signing can range from $100-$200. While there may be a slowdown in demand for notary services due to the current real estate market, I haven't ruled out this option for the future.

Tutoring online is another possibility for retirees looking to supplement their income. With so many students learning these days remotely, the demand for online tutors has grown significantly. If you have expertise in a particular subject area, you could earn extra money by offering services through one of the many online tutoring platforms.

I've also considered copywriting as a potential income stream. Having edited many teacher reports in my previous job, I've gained some writing skills that could be used well. Plenty of online training and resources are available for aspiring copywriters, and many agencies that hire remote workers in this field. While writing samples may be required as part of the application process, it's a great way to put your skills to use and earn some extra money in retirement.

Retirement is a time to embrace new opportunities and explore different paths. I don't want to sit back and watch life pass me by when I retire. I want to take control of my financial future and find fulfilling work that allows me to share my passions and knowledge with others.

One option I considered was a social media business. It's a great way to reach a broad audience and share your expertise on a particular topic. I want to develop a curriculum to share the facets of my life that could educate other women about healthy aging. I had a plan, but I knew it would take time to develop an income. However, I still keep it up my sleeve for the future.

Another option that resonated with me was health and lifestyle coaching. I had completed a health coach certificate program and had previously owned a health foods store with my husband. It felt like a natural fit for me to share my knowledge on healthy aging with others. However, I knew that to make it financially viable, I would need to address groups through social media rather than single clients.

Real estate investing also piqued my interest, but I knew I needed to develop another option first to make it happen. Renting out my own home and living temporarily in a different situation was a possibility to save money to invest in more properties.

Ultimately, the option that spoke to me the loudest was book writing and self-publishing.

It was my Eureka moment!

Writing a book had been suggested to me at different times. During the pandemic, the demand for books increased, especially with the easy availability of Kindle and audiobooks. I could share my knowledge and experience on healthy aging and reach a broad audience through self-publishing on Amazon KDP.

There are other options available, which I have not dabbled in but that you might benefit from.

If you're crafty or have a product you've developed, consider selling it online. Websites like Etsy or Amazon Handmade make it easy to set up a shop and start selling.

If you love animals, pet sitting or dog walking can be a great way to earn extra income. You can offer your services to friends and family or advertise your services on websites such as Rover or Care.com.

If you have expertise in a particular field, you can offer your services as a consultant. You can offer consulting services on a freelance basis or work with consulting firms.

You can rent it out on Airbnb if you have extra space in your home. This can be a great source of income, especially if you live in a popular tourist destination.

These are just a few examples of alternative income streams you can explore.

The secret is finding something you enjoy that fits your skills and interests.

Remember, retirement can be a time of creativity and exploration, and finding new ways to generate income can be a fulfilling and rewarding experience.

I know that exploring alternative income streams can be intimidating, especially when you're unsure where to start. Taking control of your financial future and embracing a creative retirement mindset is important. Don't be afraid to explore new opportunities and find work that brings you fulfillment in your retirement.

Well, my fellow retirees, we've covered a lot of ground today.

From Furnished Finder to Notary Public, from Online Tutoring to Copywriting, from Social Media Business to Health Coaching, and from Real Estate Investing to Book Writing and Self-Publishing, we've discussed various options for generating income in retirement.

As we've seen, retirement doesn't mean we have to stop working or earning money altogether. We can embrace a productive mindset and find new ways to use our skills and knowledge to make a meaningful contribution to society and secure our financial future.

I want to leave you with a quote from the book "Retirement Reinvention: Make Your Next Act Your Best Act" by Robin Ryan.

She writes,

"Retirement is a time to reinvent yourself. It is the perfect opportunity to rediscover what you love to do and find ways to turn that passion into a paying job."

So, let's say yes to this new phase of life with enthusiasm and optimism. Let's stay curious, keep learning, and continue discovering all the possibilities of retirement. Who knows, we may just uncover our true calling and find fulfillment in ways we never imagined.

Cheers to a rewarding and prosperous retirement!

Chapter 4:
Getting Started

Have you ever planted a seed and watched it grow?

Whether it's a tiny sprout or a flourishing plant, there's something magical about witnessing growth and change. The same can be said for creating a new experience for yourself, especially regarding retirement.

In her book, *"You Can Heal Your Life,"* Louise L. Hay uses the metaphor of a tomato plant to explain the process of growth and manifestation. She reminds us that just like a tomato plant, creating a new experience for ourselves starts with a tiny seed. It may not look like much at first, but that tiny seed can grow into something unique with suitable soil, water, and sunshine.

How?

Picture a healthy tomato plant loaded with over a hundred juicy tomatoes. Believe it or not, that tomato plant started as a tiny, dry seed. If you didn't know any better, you wouldn't even think that tiny seed could become a plant, let alone a plant with so many delicious tomatoes.

That seed was planted in fertile soil, watered, and exposed to sunshine. And as soon as that first tiny shoot appeared, the gardener didn't stomp on it and say,

"That's not a tomato plant. No way!"

They looked at it with delight and said, *"Oh boy, here it comes!"* And that little plant was nurtured with care, the weeds were pulled, and it grew into a beautiful, bountiful tomato plant.

Now, what does this have to do with retirement, you ask?

Well, creating a fulfilling retirement is a lot like growing a tomato plant. It all starts with a tiny seed - a new idea, an opportunity, or a desire to change. You plant that seed in the soil of your subconscious mind, water it with positive affirmations, and let the sunshine of your creative thoughts beam on it.

And just like that little tomato plant, you don't stomp on the first breakthrough you see. Instead, you celebrate and nurture it carefully, pulling out negative thoughts like pesky weeds.

Before you know it, that tiny seed of an idea can grow into a fulfilling and abundant retirement full of joy, purpose, and financial security.

But where do you even begin?

It can be tempting to put it off, thinking that retirement is still years away. But the truth is, it's never too early to start planning for your future. Scaling back on your 8-hour job, even just a little bit, can give you the time to start researching and making plans. And trust me, you'll be grateful for that head start when the financial crunch hits.

Don't let the fear of the unknown keep you from taking control of your financial future. Embrace a creative and exploratory mindset, and remember that every journey starts with a single step. And that first step is as simple as planting that tiny seed of intention.

So, you're ready to embark on your retirement journey but not quite sure where to start.

One option that comes to mind is using job search engines to find part-time or remote work that aligns with your expertise and interests. While this can be a great way to supplement your retirement income and stay active in the workforce, there are a few things to remember.

In full disclosure, be prepared to receive a lot of job listings that are not a good fit for you.

It's almost like these sites are playing a game of "let's see how many irrelevant jobs we can send this person's way."

Although you carefully enter your qualifications and preferred work structure, many job search engines still send you a wide range of job postings that do not meet your criteria. Sifting through these irrelevant listings can be frustrating, but don't let it discourage you.

Keep searching and refining your search criteria until you find jobs that are a good fit.

In fact, many retirement experts recommend using job search engines as a starting point but not relying solely on them.

In his book, "Retire Early: What Are You Waiting for?" author Eric Gaddy emphasizes the importance of networking and creating your job opportunities. He writes,

"By developing relationships and exploring opportunities, you'll have a better chance of finding work that aligns with your values and interests."

While job search engines can be a valuable resource, it's important to keep an open mind and consider alternative methods for finding work in retirement. Also, be sure to research and thoroughly vet any job listings that interest you.

Let's now talk about the power of social media. And the repercussions.

Social media is not just for millennials and Gen Z-ers. It's for retirees too! And the best part is that you don't have to spend a penny learning how to use it effectively.

You may wonder, *"Why do I need to learn social media now that I'm retired?"*

My dear friend, social media can help you in many ways. For one, it can help you stay connected with family and friends, especially if you live far away. It can also help you stay updated with news and current events. And if you're planning to start a business or a side hustle in retirement, social media can be a powerful tool for marketing and promoting your brand.

I know social media can be intimidating, especially if you're not tech-savvy.

But fear not!

There are plenty of free seminars and workshops out there that can teach you the ropes. Some organizations, like **AARP** and **SCORE**, explicitly offer free social media classes for retirees.

You can also check with your local library or community center to see if they offer classes or workshops.

Attending a free social media seminar can be a fun and educational experience. Not only will you learn how to navigate different social media platforms, but you'll also have the opportunity to connect with other retirees who are also learning the ropes. And who knows, you might even make some new friends!

I know some of you may be skeptical about the benefits of social media. You may be thinking, *"I don't need social media. I'm perfectly happy without it."*

And that's totally fine!

But before you dismiss social media altogether, I encourage you to keep an open mind and consider the possibilities.

As retirement expert Kerry Hannon says in her book "Great Jobs for Everyone 50+,"

"Social media has changed the way we communicate and do business. For those who take the time to learn how to use it effectively, the rewards can be enormous."

So, don't be afraid to dip your toes into social media, but don't be gullible either.

Let me explain to you why.

That infamous pitch at the end of a free seminar.

Imagine this scenario—you sign up for a free seminar, eagerly anticipating some new knowledge or opportunity, only to be bombarded with pitches to join an online course or buy a product at the end.

What do you do?

Here are some practical solutions.

Firstly, sign up for as many free seminars as you can. You never know what opportunity might present itself, and attending these seminars is a great way to expand your knowledge and explore different income opportunities.

When you attend these seminars, take copious notes. Try to absorb as much information as possible, and don't be afraid to ask questions if something doesn't quite make sense.

But when the pitch at the end comes, ignore it if it's not something that interests you or that you can't afford. You don't have to sign up for every course or buy every product. It's okay to be selective.

Remember that the seminar host is likely trying to make a living from their expertise, and there's nothing wrong with that.

But if you're hesitant to sign up for their course or buy their product, there are other ways to access their knowledge. For example, try Googling the presenter's name. They may have written books containing much or most of the seminar content they are selling.

If you do decide to sign up for the course, make sure you do your due diligence. Research the presenter and the course before committing, and ensure it aligns with your interests and goals.

For example, let's say you attend a free seminar on starting a small business. The presenter is engaging and informative, and you feel you've learned much.

At the end of the seminar, the presenter pitches a six-week online course on small business management for $500. You're not sure if you want to spend that kind of money, but you research the presenter and find out that they've written a book on small business management that covers much of the same material as the course.

You decide to buy the book for $20 and read through it, and you feel like you've gained a lot of valuable knowledge without breaking the bank.

Ultimately, signing up for a course or buying a product is totally up to you.

If it's something you're interested in and can afford, go for it!

But don't feel like you have to buy every product or sign up for every course pitched to you at a free seminar. Do your research, trust your gut, and make decisions that resonate with your financial journey.

Attend that free seminar, learn the ropes, and see where it takes you. Who knows, you might discover a whole new world of possibilities.

Retirement expert Ernie Zelinski advises in his book, "How to Retire Happy, Wild, and Free,"

"Be wary of any job opportunity that requires a large upfront investment or seems too good to be true."

This brings us to something that nobody likes to experience – *scams.*

Unfortunately, as we search for income opportunities, we'll encounter plenty of people eager to separate us from our hard-earned cash.

I speak from experience.

Yes, unfortunately, I fell victim to a scam. I signed up to be trained as an "advertising agent" for corporate businesses that promised fabulous returns.

But as it turned out, the whole thing was a sham. I lost $37, but luckily, I didn't fall for any additional options they offered. Looking back, I could see that every review I read would have warned me about this scam, but I didn't take the time to do my research.

So, my advice is to always check consumer feedback before paying to join any seminar or course. With the internet at our fingertips, it's never been easier to find reviews and feedback from other people who have gone through the same experience. Don't just rely on the reviews on the company's website. Check out independent review sites and social media platforms to get a more accurate picture.

Another tip is to be wary of anyone who promises you'll get rich quickly.

As the old saying goes, it probably is if it sounds too good to be true. Be cautious of anyone who promises that you can make a lot of money with little effort or time investment.

Real wealth takes time and effort to build, and there's no such thing as a get-rich-quick scheme. Don't fall prey to that mentality.

If I haven't mentioned this already, *trust your gut.*

It probably is if something doesn't feel right or seems too good to be true. Don't be pressured into making a decision on the spot; always take the time to do your investigation.

It's important to remember that not all income opportunities are created equal. Don't let the fear of scams hold you back from tapping into new opportunities, but don't let your excitement blind you to potential red flags.

Retirement is often seen as a time of endings, but I see it as a time of new beginnings. It's an opportunity to explore new interests and hobbies, travel to new places, and connect with loved ones in a deeper way.

And just like planting a seed, it all starts with getting started.

This is exactly why we need to assess our current financial situation and create a plan that will allow us to live comfortably in retirement. This may involve saving more, investing wisely, and making intelligent financial decisions.

But financial planning is just the beginning. Retirement is also a time to nurture new interests and passions. Maybe you've always wanted to learn a new language or take up painting. Or perhaps you're interested in volunteering or mentoring younger generations.

Whatever it may be, it's important to embrace a creative, exploratory mindset and take advantage of retirement opportunities.

Of course, like any journey, there may be obstacles along the way. Negative thoughts and self-doubt can creep in, causing us to doubt ourselves and our abilities. But just like pulling weeds from a garden, we need to actively work to remove these negative thoughts and replace them with positive affirmations and a can-do attitude.

And when we see even the tiniest bit of progress, we should celebrate it with enthusiasm and joy. Celebrate your growth and personal wins by patting yourself on the back.

So, let's plant that seed and watch it grow with optimism. May your harvest be plentiful, your financial future secure, and your retirement years filled with joy, adventure, and contentment.

Stay smart and stay safe out there!

Chapter 5:
Is This The Right Fit?

We've covered a lot of ground so far, from discovering alternate income streams to overcoming the fear of getting started and finding a new sense of purpose in retirement.

Now, we will explore one of the most exciting aspects of retirement: finding a work opportunity that is the perfect fit for you.

When it comes to work in retirement, the possibilities are truly endless. Some retirees continue working in their current field, while others opt for a different career path.

What is important to remember is to find something that truly speaks to your passions and interests. After all, retirement is the perfect time to pursue those hobbies and activities you've always dreamed of doing.

As the great Elizabeth Gilbert once said, *"You can live a long life, making and doing really cool things the entire time…And at the end of your days, you can thank creativity for having blessed you with a charmed, interesting, passionate existence."*

Finding the right fit for your post-retirement work life can seem like a mammoth task, but it doesn't have to be. You can start exploring your options by looking at your hobbies and interests.

Is there a particular activity that you've always enjoyed and excelled at?

Maybe it's painting, writing, gardening, or even cooking. Now is the time to turn that hobby into a fulfilling and profitable venture.

You can also consider part-time work in a field you're passionate about. For example, consider working part-time at your local golf course. Not only will you be able to enjoy your hobby, but you'll also earn a little extra income in the process.

When finding the right fit, it's essential to keep an open mind and not be afraid to try new things. Retirement is the perfect time to explore new opportunities and take risks.

Maya Angelou once said, *"Pursue the things you love doing and then do them so well that people can't take their eyes off you."*

Many retirees make the mistake of simply looking for any job that will pay the bills, but finding work that brings you joy and satisfaction can make a huge difference in your overall well-being.

So, how can you find the right fit for you?

Think about your strengths and weaknesses.

What activities make you feel most fulfilled and energized? Do you enjoy working with people or prefer to work independently?

Are you looking for a job that allows you to be creative or requires more structure?

These are all essential considerations to keep in mind as you explore your options.

Consider your skills and experience.

What are you good at? What have you done in the past that you enjoyed or excelled at?

Remember, just because you're retired doesn't mean you don't have valuable skills and experience to offer.

Remember that finding the right fit may take some time and experimentation.

Trying different jobs and seeing what works best for you is okay. Trial and error is the way to go. To be honest, some of the most successful retirees I know have tried several jobs before finding the one that genuinely pleased them.

Finding the right job opportunity that aligns with your skillset can be a formidable task, especially in retirement. But don't worry. It's never too late to turn your hobby into a profitable idea.

As Elizabeth Gilbert said in her book Big Magic: Creative Living Beyond Fear, *"Once you put your expression and passion behind an idea, that idea becomes yours."*

I have an exercise for you to help you brainstorm some great ideas. Answer these questions on a piece of paper:

1. What do you love to do? What interests you? What are you passionate about?

It doesn't matter if it's related to a job or not. Just focus on what you love.

2. *What are your unique gifts and talents? What do people thank you for or come to you for help with?*

These can be valuable skills that you may not even realize you have.

3. *What skills do you want to use?*

Think about the actions you want to take regularly and how you want to spend your day.

4. *What industries are interesting to you?*

Research and talk to people in those industries to learn more about them.

5. What values do you want to express through your work? Money is great, but what motivates you beyond that? Do you want to give back, be creative, or have every day be different?

6. Who are you? No, Really?

Matching your personality type to a job is vital for happiness and success.

7. What kind of work environment are you looking for?

Think about the type of culture you work best in and what's most important to you.

8. What is your mission? What are you compelled to do in life? What do you want to be remembered for?

9. What is your ideal salary?

Knowing what you need to make can help determine what jobs you can consider.

Once you have the answers, you'll have a good sense of what you're looking for, use advanced search techniques, and network with people in your desired industry to find opportunities.

Don't be afraid to ask for help or recommendations, and be on the lookout for new job opportunities.

Retirement is a time that many people look forward to, but it can also be a time of uncertainty, especially if you don't have enough money to maintain your standard of living.

According to the Boston College Center for Retirement Research, only half of all pre-retirement households have enough assets to do so.

As Elizabeth Gilbert points out, *"A lot of people don't know exactly what their passion is, or they may have multiple passions, or they may be going through a midlife change of passion, all of which can leave them feeling confused and blocked and insecure."*

Agreed!

But you know what they say: life begins at 40, 50, 60, or 70. Life begins whenever you want it to start. The truth is, it's never too late to discover new passions or reignite old ones.

Sometimes, figuring out what sets our soul on fire can feel overwhelming.

Maybe we have multiple interests and feel pulled in different directions, or perhaps we're experiencing a midlife crisis, questioning everything we thought we knew about ourselves.

Whatever the case may be, Elizabeth Gilbert reminds us that it's okay to feel confused or unsure about our passions.

The important thing is to keep moving forward, working steadily, and trusting that creativity will always find us, even when we've lost sight of it.

When we have a creative and exploratory mindset, we give ourselves the freedom to try new things, experiment, and follow our curiosities wherever they lead us.

You must widen your search and use your own unique life experiences and creativity to seek new sources of income.

You may just discover a passion you never knew you had!

There are some things you can do to take control of your financial future and make the most of your retirement years.

Retirement and work are not as black and white as they used to be. Many Americans who are 65 years old and working had retired at some point in the past and then returned to the workforce, according to research from the *Rand Institute.*

So, if you're anxious about getting back into the game, don't worry. You're not alone.

You don't have to hold out for a nine-to-five office job with benefits. Research shows that even working an hourly job for a few extra years, plus delaying Social Security if possible, can boost your retirement security.

It's common for older workers to worry that they can't compete in the labor market. But the truth is, older workers don't look all that different from their younger counterparts.

While studies show that older workers may have a more challenging time mastering new information quickly, there is little-to-no evidence that someone's existing knowledge, verbal or word skills are impaired by age.

So, have confidence in your abilities!

You have a wealth of experience to draw upon when taking on new challenges, which may even give you a leg-up on younger workers. Believing in your ability to affect the world around you, especially regarding finances positively, can improve your circumstances.

If you struggled during the pandemic, don't worry; you're not alone. Many older workers took time out of the workforce due to parenting, caregiving, or other necessities.

The lesson is not to dwell on it but confidently explain your story. Update your LinkedIn profile, reach out to your network telling them you're interested in work, and update your resume to include the skills relevant to the new position you're considering.

The pandemic upended the lives of millions of near-retirees, but if you weren't ready to hang up your spurs completely, now is the time to re-engage.

I recently had the fortune of reading about a study by Indeed.com that identified the most popular part-time jobs for Americans aged 62 and up.

And guess what?

Driving jobs and medical jobs topped the list.

Who wouldn't want to be a van driver or telemedicine physician in their golden years?

But if that's not your cup of tea, don't worry. I did some digging and found out that there are plenty of other options out there.

Andrew Flowers, an economist at Indeed Hiring Lab, shared another study that identified the top 50 part-time jobs with the most postings over the past two years.

And, surprise, surprise, healthcare jobs were still on the list, along with retail, hospitality, and teaching jobs.

Susan K. Weinstock, the vice president for financial resilience at **AARP**, also chimed in and said that **AARP's** jobs board had plenty of listings for retail and hospitality jobs and call-center customer service jobs.

Now, here's the thing.

Just because a job sector has a lot of openings doesn't mean it's the best fit for you.

You need to think about what you want and need out of a job in retirement.

Do you want to earn extra income, meet new people, or keep yourself busy?

And don't forget to consider any limitations you might have, like being unable to work weekends or stand for long periods.

Here are some tips to help you jump-start your part-time job search:

1. Reach out to former employers and colleagues.

They might have the perfect part-time job for you.

2. Volunteer.

If you prove your skills and attitude, it could lead to a paid part-time position.

3. Check out job boards for those aged 50 and over, like AARP's jobs board, Retirementjobs.com, and Retiredbrains.com.

4. Look for job boards specializing in part-time, seasonal, and flexible jobs, like *Coolworks.com* and *FlexJobs.com.*

5. Don't forget to look locally. Check out places like libraries, schools, and community arts centers for part-time job openings.

As we end this chapter, I want to leave you with another moving quote from Elizabeth Gilbert's book "Big Magic: Creative Living Beyond Fear."

Gilbert is speaking about her creative pursuits, but I believe her words apply just as much to our quest for financial security in retirement. She writes,

"But I don't sit around waiting for passion to strike me. I keep working steadily because I believe it is our privilege as humans to keep making things for as long as we live and because I enjoy making things. Most of all, I keep working because I trust that creativity is always trying to find me, even when I have lost sight of it."

This quote teaches us that we must actively participate in our financial future. We can't sit around waiting for a windfall or a brilliant idea to fall into our laps. We must keep working steadily, exploring new avenues of income, and tapping into our creativity and unique life experiences.

I know it's not always easy, but it's a privilege to keep making things, whether creating a new business, writing a book, or even exploring a new hobby.

So, I advise you to widen your search for income opportunities and tap into your creativity and unique experiences.

Don't be afraid to take risks and try new things. And remember, even when you feel like you've lost sight of your creativity or your financial future seems uncertain, trust that it's always trying to find you.

With hard work and a positive mindset, you can take control of your financial future and create a secure retirement that's as rewarding as it is.

Chapter 6:
Narrowing the Focus

Let's continue on our journey to finding the perfect side hustle in retirement. It's important to remember that the process can be overwhelming at times. With so many opportunities out there, narrowing down our focus and finding the right fit for us can be difficult.

But don't fret because your intuition is your greatest tool in this process.

Caroline Myss, a renowned author and speaker on spirituality and intuition, once said,

"We often hesitate to follow our intuition out of fear. Most usually, we are afraid of the changes in our own lives that our actions will bring. Intuitive guidance, however, is all about change. It is energetic data ripe with the potential to influence the rest of the world. To fear change but to crave intuitive clarity is like fearing the cold, dark night while pouring water on the fire that lights your cave. An insight the size of a mustard seed is powerful enough to bring down a mountain-sized illusion that may be holding our lives together. Truth strikes without mercy. We fear our intuitions because we fear the transformational power within our revelations."

Remember, when presented with new opportunities or changes, it's easy to feel hesitant and uncertain. But intuition is powerful and can guide us towards the right path, even if it may lead to some discomfort or change.

You are a retiree with the advantage of life experience and wisdom, which can help you refine your intuition and make sound decisions.

When investigating potential side hustles, it's important to trust your gut instincts and explore all options that come your way. Don't be afraid to try something new and step outside your comfort zone.

For example, if you've always had a passion for photography but never pursued it professionally, don't hesitate to explore the possibility of starting a photography business. You may be surprised at the opportunities that arise when you investigate your interests and follow your intuition.

It's also important to remember that narrowing your focus doesn't mean limiting yourself.

Truthfully, by using your intuition and investigating all options, you may uncover new and exciting opportunities you never even considered before.

If I haven't said this already, let me tell you something: retirement doesn't mean you're done with life.

It's just the opposite!

Retirement is the perfect time to explore, learn, and try new things. And if you're worried about money, don't be. There are so many opportunities out there to create income in retirement. You just have to be open to them.

Intuition is your best friend.

Do you know that gut feeling you get sometimes? The one that tells you to take a chance on something or to avoid a specific situation?

That's your intuition, and it's a powerful tool for exploring income options in retirement.

I can't stress enough how important it is to trust your gut and investigate all options that come your way. There are no accidents in life. Pay attention, whether it's an algorithm sending a particular training your way or running into a friend who describes what another friend is doing.

These are all signs that could lead you to your next big opportunity.

For example, let's say you're scrolling through social media and see an ad for an online course about starting a side hustle.

You might initially feel hesitant, but if your intuition tells you to check it out, don't ignore that feeling.

Investigate the course, read reviews, and see if it aligns with your interests and skills. You never know. That course could lead to a successful side hustle that brings in some extra income.

Maybe you're at a party and overhear a conversation about someone making money by selling handmade crafts online.

Again, listen to your intuition.

If you feel a spark of interest, ask that person more about their experience. Follow that trail. Who knows, maybe you have a talent for crafting and could turn it into a profitable business.

When looking for a job, it's essential to trust your intuition as a valid source of information. Interviewers often put the company's very best foot forward, and that's fine, but authenticity can be lacking.

Pay close attention to all the signals you're getting when you walk into the building, including people's body language.

Take all that into account, not only whatever is in the formal job description, and listen to your intuition about whether you'd want to work there every day.

Intuition is a powerful tool for decision-making, and it can be the tie-breaker in your pro and con list.

It can also be the easiest path to deciding if something is right for you. If you want to strengthen your intuition when it comes to making career decisions, I want you to start with these tips:

Know yourself.

Listen to your inner voice.

Tune into your body.

Trust yourself.

Be patient.

Release control and the need to be right.

And finally,

Continue to pay attention to what happens when you listen to your intuition.

Trust that you already have the answer within you. Be open to receiving the signs without judging, and trust that you can handle anything.

Remember, if you're patient and release the need to control every outcome, you'll find that using your intuition to explore new sources of income will be the most rewarding experience ever.

Here, I would like to talk about a worthwhile skill that would help you align your goals and make your retirement fruitful.

Time management. Let me explain why.

Retirement can be an exciting time full of newfound freedom and endless possibilities. Finally, you can say goodbye to the days of punching a time clock and embrace the creative and exploratory mindset that comes with retirement. But with all this newfound freedom, it can be easy to lose track of time and feel disoriented without work and family structure.

That's why it's essential to have some schedule in retirement.

Don't worry. You don't have to block out every minute of the day rigorously!

Time management in retirement is more about setting goals and priorities and ensuring you accomplish what you set out to do.

Here are some practical tips on how to manage your time in retirement without feeling like you're back on the clock:

1. Take Things into Perspective

Remember that time management in retirement is not about over-managing your schedule or feeling like every minute of the day needs to be scheduled. It's more about setting goals and priorities and making sure that you accomplish what you set out to do.

2. Make A Schedule

Organize your activities daily or weekly, not hour by hour. This way, you can plan to exercise on Tuesdays and Thursdays, have a class on Wednesdays, and play cards on Fridays without feeling like you're rushing from one activity to the next.

3. Make A List

Some people are planners, while others are more freeform. Whatever your personality, it's helpful to list the important things or the things you need to get out of the way. This way, you can wake up knowing what you need to accomplish, which can help you sleep better at night.

4. Be Flexible

You might not need a schedule for everyday chores like housekeeping or gardening. Instead, just tackle a few tasks when you're ready, knowing it will all be done in the end. Permit yourself to move an activity from today's list to tomorrow, next week, or even never if you realize it's something you don't want to do.

5. Learn to Slow Down

It's easy to feel anxious about all your free time in retirement, so you might be tempted to fill your days with busy work. But busy work eats up time without offering any sense of fulfillment. Once you accept that you don't have to be active every minute of the day, you can stop putting pressure on yourself and start accomplishing the things you want to do at your own pace.

6. Find Your Rhythm

Everyone has their daily rhythm, so find yours and follow it. If you're a morning person, take care of finances, write in your journal, and plan family vacations in the morning. Leave routine work for the afternoons and evenings. If you're a night owl, do the opposite.

7. Alternate Periods of Structured Activity with Free Time

Just like in school, when the freedom of summer vacation followed the structure of the school year, you can add texture to your retirement life by alternating periods of structured activity with free time. For example, you could enjoy the structure of regular volunteer work, a seasonal job, or taking a class, followed by a period with no obligations. And then, when you're getting bored, it's back to the routine again.

8. Limit Your Screen Time

It's easy to let electronics soak up all your time. Make a conscious choice about how much time to devote to these passive activities.

9. Take Your Weekend During the Week

Avoid lines by shopping on Monday or Tuesday instead of the weekend. You save time and enjoy more attention from salesclerks. Similarly, play golf or tennis or vacation during the week to avoid the crowds and get a cheaper rate.

Finally, remember that times change.

Your retirement needs will change over time, and that's perfectly normal. Some people begin retirement doing everything they'd been putting off, such as painting the house, going on a trip, or joining a club.

But what happens after you check off those activities?

You may want to reconsider your priorities and revise your schedule.

So, how does time management relate to finding an alternative source of income?

By creating a schedule and setting priorities, you'll have a better idea of how much time you have available for an alternative source of income. This will help you determine what gig you can realistically take on.

Let's say you want to start a side business selling handmade pottery.

You'll need to factor in the time it takes to create the pottery, glaze it, and fire it, as well as the time it takes to set up an online shop or sell it at local craft fairs.

When you map out your schedule and set aside specific times for each task, you can determine if this is a feasible side hustle for you.

Conversely, if you don't have much extra time, you might consider a job requiring less time commitment, such as dog walking or pet-sitting. These types of jobs can be done on your schedule and don't require as much prep work or setup time.

A valuable outcome of time management in retirement is that it can help you avoid burnout.

It's easy to get excited about a new side hustle and want to spend all your time on it, but this can quickly lead to exhaustion and frustration. When you set realistic goals and boundaries for yourself, you'll be able to avoid burnout and enjoy your job without it feeling like a burden.

But too much of anything can make you sick, which is the case with simultaneously taking on too many side hustles.

If you have too many options, you need to recourse and prioritize!

It's pretty tempting to get excited about opportunities and want to pursue them all. But the reality is that spreading ourselves too thin can lead to burnout and decreased productivity. We must prioritize our choices and focus on one option at a time.

Once you've decided to pursue a specific option, commit to it and give it your all. Don't let other opportunities distract you from your chosen path. If you've researched, the possibilities will remain there after you've given your all to your current pursuit.

Remember, it's okay to have multiple interests and explore different options. But taking on too much can be overwhelming and counterproductive.

So, stay focused and committed to the choice that spoke to your heart.

Still, if you are interested in dabbling in more than one source of income, here are five handy questions to ask yourself.

1. Has The Quality of Each Source of Income Gone Down?

If you're finding it hard to focus or don't have enough energy to put in your best work, it might be a sign that you have too many side hustles. If you're seeing slippages in work quality, such as less readership or comments on a product you make, it can result in less income.

2. No Time for Breaks

Breaks are important to recharge, and if you're constantly working, it can be counterproductive. While it may seem like working through your furlough is productive, it can lead to burnout and ultimately lower quality work.

3. Organization

Tax time is a great example of when organization is important. If you struggle to keep up with all the paperwork, it may be a sign that you have too much on your plate.

4. Working Hard or Hardly Working

Side hustles aim to bring in some extra money and attempt to make it passive income. However, some side hustles require more work for less money. When deciding which side hustle to prioritize, choose the one that is more passive and *"pays"* you more for your hard work.

5. Neglecting Your Source of Income

Your main job is most likely your biggest source of income, and neglecting it can have serious consequences. In some cases, focusing on getting certifications or licenses to boost your career might be more impactful than spending all your time on a side hustle that doesn't add much value.

Once you've considered these five questions, it's time to evaluate whether your side hustle is worth your time.

Don't feel bad if you need to shut down a less-than-profitable or less-enjoyable side hustle.

Think of it as a re-direction of energy and resources towards things that you want to do.

The most successful ventures are the ones that you enjoy and that reward you for your efforts. But don't be shy about going out there and making the most of your side hustles, but don't forget to prioritize and focus on what's most important!

We've covered a lot of ground on finding the right source of income in retirement, developing time management skills, and avoiding the pitfalls of taking on too many side hustles at once.

I want to conclude this chapter with one final thought.

As Caroline Myss wrote in her book Anatomy of the Spirit: The Seven Stages of Power and Healing,

"Intuition, like all meditative disciplines, can be enormously effective if and only if one has the courage and personal power to follow through on the guidance it provides."

In other words, you're taking a risk when you follow your intuition. You're stepping out of your comfort zone and into new territory, which can sometimes be uncomfortable. But it is precisely where the most significant rewards lie.

While we often measure our success in terms of our comfort and security, the universe measures our success by how much we have learned.

So, if you're feeling uncomfortable or uncertain about your retirement income plan, remember that it's all part of the learning process. Trust your intuition, act on its guidance, and focus on your priorities.

In the end, success isn't just about achieving financial security or comfort; it's about how much you've learned and how much you've grown along the way!

Chapter 7: Powerful Appreciation

"I'm retired. Does the work that I do even matter?"

Have you ever asked yourself this question?

Well, my friends, let me tell you that your work matters irrespective of what it is. Whether you're pursuing a hobby, volunteering, or tackling some major tasks at the office, everything you do holds immense value. It's like the secret ingredient that adds flavor to your life and leaves a lasting impact on those around you.

Speaking of flavors, you must have heard of the legendary Julia Child. She was a culinary genius who transformed cooking into art.

She once said, *"To be a good cook, you have to have a love of the good, hard work, and creating."*

And I believe these exact words are true for your work.

Julia published her very first cookbook when she was in her 50s.

Can you believe it?

She faced skeptics who doubted her abilities and questioned why she was starting late. But she didn't let those naysayers dampen her spirit. With unwavering determination and a pinch of audacity, she set out to conquer the culinary world.

Julia's path wasn't an easy one, and it was filled with numerous obstacles. She stumbled, burned a few dishes, and faced rejections. But she never lost her appetite for success. Instead, she embraced the challenges as opportunities for growth. She rolled up her sleeves, sharpened her skills, and poured her heart and soul into perfecting her craft.

And her hard work paid off!

Julia's perseverance and dedication made her a household name. She inspired aspiring cooks worldwide, proving that age is just a number when it comes to pursuing your passion.

So, I urge you to let Julia's journey be a guiding recipe for your path to success. Embrace the obstacles, for they are the spices adding flavor to your story. Rise above the doubts and limitations that society may impose upon you, and let your determination simmer to perfection.

Acknowledge the sweat, tears, and laughter that go into every endeavor you undertake. Be your own mentor, cheerleader, and confidant. Take a moment to pat yourself on the back to revel in the small victories that make up your remarkable journey. Your accomplishments deserve a standing ovation, my dear friends.

Remember, the fruits of your hard work are meant to be savored. With each milestone and goal accomplished, take a moment to appreciate the flavors of success. Taste the sweetness of triumph and the savory satisfaction of a well-done job.

In this chapter on powerful appreciation, I will teach you to take a step back, raise your spoon, and savor the dishes you've prepared in life. Celebrate the hurdles you've conquered and the flavors you've added to the world. Your hard work, just like Julia's, is the secret ingredient that makes life more prosperous and more meaningful.

So, how did I garner a powerful appreciation for my own work, you might wonder?

My journey in special education has shaped me in ways I never could have imagined. It taught me the art of differentiation—recognizing the difference between small and large problems.

When you work with students who can turn the tiniest frustration into a full-blown tantrum, responding rather than reacting is crucial. It's about maintaining that steady presence in the room – the calm in the storm. Over time, this approach helped me build a trust-based relationship with my students and ensure their safety.

And you know what?

These qualities have seeped into other areas of my life, too. Now, I find myself not sweating the small stuff as much. Coupled with my spiritual perspective, I can keep the bigger picture in sight and not let obstacles overwhelm me. It's like having a pair of magical glasses that allow me to see through the fog and focus on what truly matters.

But that's not all.

Working alongside a diverse group of coworkers, most of whom are from my son's generation, has been a delightful gift.

Age hardly ever becomes a factor in how we relate to one another. I blend right in, tackling tasks and engaging in interactions just like any other staff member.

Well, maybe with a touch of added respect for the wisdom I've gained over the years. It's remarkable how immersing myself in a culture that encourages youthful energy and mindset makes me forget the significant age difference that exists.

It gives me the gift of staying mentally and emotionally young. Imagine being immersed in a work environment surrounded by a younger generation with infectious energy and invigorating ideas. It's like a fountain of youth, constantly reminding us that age is just a number.

In this ever-evolving world, flexibility has become our trusted companion. It nudges us to reinvent ourselves, embrace new challenges, and explore new opportunities with open arms. The secret ingredient keeps our minds sharp, our spirits vibrant, and our hearts open to endless possibilities.

This is how, even after retiring, we know all will be well. We have the resilience, the experience, and the unwavering determination to navigate the winding paths of reinvention.

We understand that life is a magnificent rollercoaster ride of change and growth. And by welcoming this flexibility, we ensure that our lives remain vibrant and rich with colorful adventures.

Now, let's talk about life's purpose.

Oh, the joy of knowing that my work has touched and impacted countless lives!

Even after almost three decades, I still find a sense of meaningfulness in my role. Many students I work with have faced multiple school failures before joining our program. Making a positive difference in their lives fills my heart with warmth and inspiration.

And here's the icing on the cake: Now and then, I receive messages from my former students expressing their gratitude for the time I spent as their teacher. It's like a gentle reminder, a pat on the back, that the work I do truly matters. Those heartfelt messages are the fuel that keeps me going, even when I occasionally feel the weight of burnout.

This is why I insist that you appreciate the power of appreciation. It's a tongue twister, but it makes sense.

Sometimes, it's easier to see what's wrong with ourselves rather than what's right. We tend to squirm when we receive praise or compliments, not knowing how to respond without feeling self-conscious.

Flattery feels nice, but how many of us truly take it in? How many of us own it and delight in it?

It's trickier than we might think to feel positive about ourselves, and fear often plays a role.

One fear is that of setting overly high expectations. We downplay our good points to avoid disappointing others if we fall short. We're also afraid of letting go of our self-deprecating habits. Embracing our positive qualities can feel unfamiliar and strange. And then there's the fear of being perceived as vain. Nobody likes a narcissist except, well, the narcissists themselves.

But here's the thing: We can celebrate our admirable qualities in a healthy way. It's all about self-compassion. We treat ourselves with kindness, acknowledging that all people have strengths and weaknesses.

I like to call it *"self-appreciation."*

When we genuinely enjoy what's good about ourselves, without arrogance or overconfidence, we revel in our goodness.

Let's talk about kindness in self-appreciation.

Think about your friends. Would you take their positive qualities for granted without ever acknowledging them or letting them know what you appreciate about them?

Probably not.

So why do we do it to ourselves?

It's an act of self-kindness to appreciate ourselves and give sincere praise internally. We don't have to shout it from the rooftops and make ourselves or others uncomfortable. But quietly acknowledging our worth is a gift we truly deserve.

Self-appreciation also stems from recognizing the common humanity within us. It's not about considering ourselves better than others; it's about understanding that all people have goodness within them.

When we appreciate others while ignoring our own worth, we create an artificial division. But the truth is, our existence is a unique expression of the universal human condition.

As the wise Zen master Thich Nhat Hanh reminded us, *"You are a wonderful manifestation. The whole universe has come together to make your existence possible."*

So, celebrating our achievements is not self-centered; it expresses gratitude for all the factors that shaped us. It humbly honors those who have contributed to our growth.

Mindfulness plays a crucial role in self-appreciation, too.

We often get so caught up in our mistakes and flaws that we overlook our accomplishments.

When you receive a work evaluation, what grabs your attention more: the nine points of praise or the one point of criticism?

Some worry that focusing too much on our strengths might cause us to neglect areas where we need to grow. And yes, that could be a problem if we go to extremes.

But the truth is, every human being possesses positive and negative traits. It's about honoring and accepting ourselves as we truly are—no better, not worse.

We need balance and perspective to see ourselves without distortion.

William James, one of the founding fathers of Western psychology, once said that *"the deepest principle in human nature is the craving to be appreciated."*

And here's the good news: We can fulfill this essential need without depending on the approval of others. When we treat ourselves with the same kindness we extend to our good friends, we create a supportive and caring environment that helps us thrive.

Consider self-appreciation as the flip side of self-compassion. Let's acknowledge our admirable qualities, celebrate our goodness, and give ourselves the love and approval we deserve.

Remember, it's not about being perfect or better than anyone else—it's about honoring our unique selves and expressing gratitude for the journey that brought us here.

Now, I want you to repeat some affirmations that will fill our hearts with gratitude and appreciation for who we are.

And remember, we're not looking for perfection here.

It's about recognizing and cherishing our unique qualities and experiences.

Here we go:

- I am grateful for the way I have supported myself. Whether managing finances, maintaining a home, or navigating life's challenges, I've done a good job.
- I am grateful for my good qualities. Maybe I have a great sense of humor that brings joy to others or a compassionate nature that helps me connect with those in need. These qualities make me special.
- I am grateful that I can rely on myself. I've weathered storms and overcome obstacles, and that's something to be proud of. I've got my own back!
- I am grateful for how I have grown through the years. Each passing year has brought wisdom, knowledge, and a deeper understanding of myself and the world around me. I'm like a fine wine, getting better with age.
- I am grateful for all the little achievements I make every day. Whether it's finishing a crossword puzzle, trying a new recipe, or simply getting out of bed with a smile, these small victories matter.

- I am grateful for the positive impact I make on the world. Maybe I volunteer at a local charity, lend a listening ear to a needy friend, or simply brighten someone's day with a kind word. Every act of kindness creates ripples of goodness.

- I am grateful to be me. There's no one else quite like me in this vast universe, and that's something truly remarkable. I bring a unique perspective, a special spark that enriches the tapestry of life.

- I am grateful for my kind heart. My capacity to love, care, and show empathy is a gift that touches the lives of those around me. It's a superpower!

- I am grateful for my body and all that it lets me do. Sure, it may not be as sprightly as it once was, but it still carries me through each day, allowing me to enjoy life's precious moments.

- I am grateful for my good health. Having the energy and vitality to savor life's adventures is something to treasure. So, cheers to staying active and feeling good!

- Lastly, I am grateful for my life. Each day is a new chapter – an opportunity to learn, grow, and create beautiful memories. Life may have thrown its curveballs, but here I am, thriving and embracing every precious moment.

Let us be grateful for the opportunity to make a difference, regardless of age. Our work has the potential to impact lives, inspire, and uplift. And in that recognition, we find the strength to be bold, to seek new livelihoods, and to continue making a real difference in the world and changing lives even though we might not know it.

You have the wisdom, experience, and passion for creating a legacy that will be cherished for future generations.

Your work matters, and it deserves to be honored!

Chapter 8: Growth Mindset

Please grab a cup of herbal tea and settle in because I am about to share my advent in the world of wellness and how it pushed me to develop a growth mindset.

It all started when I packed my bags and embarked on a grand adventure with my husband. We left sunny California and found ourselves in beautiful Colorado.

And guess what?

Fate had a surprise in store for us. We stumbled upon a small health food store in Greeley, and before we knew it, we were managing the place.

Can you believe it?

Back then, terms like "organically grown" and "whole grain" were met with raised eyebrows and chuckles. We saw the potential in those funny-sounding words.

Our little store quickly became the buzzing heart of the community, drawing in a growing tribe of health enthusiasts, or as some liked to call us, *"health nuts."*

We were like the Pied Pipers of good nutrition, leading the way to a healthier lifestyle.

We even dabbled in biodynamic farming and gardening. How did that happen?

A wonderful family who frequented our store introduced us to the magic of biodynamic practices. It was like stepping into a whole new world of sustainable living.

Fast forward a bit, and we lived and worked on a biodynamic farm in Germany for a year.

Can you imagine the pastoral rawness?

We were knee-deep in soil, nurturing the earth and growing our food. It was a transformative experience that ignited a lifelong commitment to staying connected to the latest nutritional research and embracing a natural way of life.

Recently, I decided to expand my knowledge and pursue a Health Coaching certification. I wanted to delve deeper into wellness and find ways to share my passion with others. So, armed with my newfound expertise, I'm currently exploring how I can turn this background into a fulfilling source of income. The possibilities are endless, and I'm excited to see where this path takes me.

I also ventured into the world of yoga. I completed not just one but two different yoga teacher training. For four glorious years, I taught yoga to the local community, spreading the joy of movement and mindfulness.

The best part is that I'm still at it. I continue to study and practice various fitness and movement plans, always eager to expand my repertoire and keep my body and mind in tip-top shape.

Now, let me share a little secret with you. In this age of technology, where Instagram reigns supreme, I've discovered some wonderful accounts that inspire me in health and fitness.

You know, those little squares of motivation that pop up on your screen?

Well, I've found a few favorites. If you're looking for a dose of positivity and inspiration, check out *@lifewithkate*, *@petrafishermovement*, *@thejoyformula*, *@heyloa*, and *@vanja.moves*.

Trust me! They'll brighten up your feed and spark that fire within to embrace a healthy lifestyle.

So, how did I develop a growth mindset?

To answer this question, I must first let you in on the secret of visualization and manifestation.

I want you to picture yourself engaging in meditation and visualization practices, focusing on affirming and manifesting the life you desire rather than allowing fear and anxiety to steer your attention toward obstacles and problems.

Pema Chödrön, a renowned meditation master and one of the foremost students of Chögyam Trungpa, offers valuable insights into this transformative phenomenon.

She speaks to the wounded, hurt, and broken parts within us, helping us develop resilience in the face of adversity and cultivate a deeper appreciation for the present moment. Drawing upon her confrontations with crisis and a wide range of Buddhist concepts and strategies, Chödrön guides us to embrace the unknown, befriend our fears, and let go of hope.

Chödrön's teachings emphasize the importance of staying with the shakiness, learning to relax amidst the chaos, and not succumbing to panic. Just as she experienced a moment of *limitless stillness* when facing her husband's affair, we too can discover opportunities for growth and transformation within our financial unpreparedness for retirement.

To manifest the life we want, Chödrön encourages us to become intimate with fear and to recognize it as a universal experience. Rather than avoiding or numbing our fears, we can embrace them and observe them without judgment.

Because once we do that, we tap into a deeper level of self-awareness and compassion, allowing us to be present with all our emotions, including wonder, awe, and joy.

Letting go of hope is another essential aspect of Chödrön's teachings. Instead of clinging to hope and always seeking a better future, we can embrace the present moment, finding joy and connection in the here and now. Once we release the attachment to outcomes, we open ourselves up to a more honest and authentic life experience.

Chödrön also introduces the practice of loving-kindness, known as *Maitri*, which involves extending unconditional friendship and compassion towards ourselves.

This practice is the foundation for developing compassion towards others, enabling us to recognize and alleviate their suffering. Through meditation and compassion-based approaches like Tonglen, we can transform our relationship with pain and difficulties into opportunities for growth and awakening.

Manifestation is a powerful tool that empowers us to create our future. When we focus on what we want and actively work toward our goals, we can transform our dreams into reality. Our thoughts and beliefs play a significant role in manifesting what we desire. They generate vibrations that impact our ability to reach our goals.

When we visualize and normalize the future we desire, we can change our frequency, just like tuning a radio, and shift our aspirations towards us.

To manifest our desires, it's imperative to know what we want and visualize it in detail regularly.

When we imagine the future we desire, we strengthen our belief that it will come to fruition. This unwavering belief becomes a magnet, attracting opportunities and encounters that can help us realize our dreams.

A clear vision and self-belief are essential components of achieving our goals through manifestation. We need to brainwash ourselves into wholeheartedly believing that our vision will come to pass. Alongside belief, we must develop a strategy and create a detailed plan to reach our goals. This involves breaking down our larger goals into smaller, manageable increments. Through this proactive approach, we can make significant progress toward our dreams.

Creating a strategy and taking action are the building blocks of the manifestation process. The law of attraction goes hand in hand with the law of action. It's not enough to merely believe and visualize; we must also work hard, establish productive habits, and take concrete steps toward our desired future.

We can create a definitive plan to work with focus and intention by chunking our vision into yearly, monthly, weekly, and daily goals.

Manifesting our ideal life follows a three-step process: vision, strategy, and action. We need to visualize our ideal life consistently, aligning our inner frequency with it. Next, we develop a detailed plan that outlines the steps required to achieve our goals. Finally, we take action, immersing ourselves in environments where we can find the relationships and opportunities we seek.

Remember, the key to manifestation lies within us. When we take action and make our dreams a reality, we shape our own lives and have the power to impact others positively. Spreading kindness, attracting positive energy, and achieving success become natural byproducts of our manifestation journey.

The Law of Attraction

Oprah, the television queen, the embodiment of success, once wanted something badly. And guess what?

She used the Law of Attraction to make it happen! Oprah believed, visualized, and worked her way toward her dream.

She got her first film role in a movie she had been dreaming about for ages. Talk about attracting what you want, right?

Oprah isn't just blowing hot air when she talks about the Law of Attraction and that famous documentary "The Secret." She firmly believes that our thoughts and choices shape our circumstances, and rightly so.

Our thoughts and actions are like the architects of our lives. If we stay positive, manifest our desires, and visualize our dreams and goals, there's a good chance we can actually turn them into reality.

Now, here's the catch. If we constantly dwell on negativity and feed those negative thoughts, guess what we attract?

Yep, you guessed it – more of the same negativity! It's like the universe is saying, *"Oh, you want more of that? Here you go."*

So, let's make a pact, my friends. Let's focus on the positive and good thoughts to attract what we truly desire.

I'm not here to sugarcoat things.

The Law of Attraction isn't some magic wand that grants every wish. It's more like a guide that shows us how to make the most out of life. We still need to take action and put in some elbow grease. Just like Oprah, we've got to believe in ourselves, visualize our goals, and work toward them. That's when the real magic happens.

If I adopt a positive image of myself, a healthy version, no matter the age, that is what I will attract.

Let's pivot into fitness, shall we?

Fitness is about keeping our bodies moving and never giving in to those pesky aches, pains, and loss of function that society tells us are just a part of aging.

Well, I'm here to tell you we're not buying it!

Exercise and yoga are the magic potions that keep us feeling like superheroes, no matter our age.

Trust me, it's like discovering the fountain of youth!

So, why should we make exercise a daily ritual? Besides the fact that it makes us feel like rock stars, it has some serious benefits when it comes to aging gracefully.

Let's break it down, shall we?

First off, exercise boosts our immune system. Imagine having the immune system of a sprightly young adult when you're rocking your retirement years. Sounds pretty awesome, right?

Well, studies have shown that folks who regularly exercise, like those incredible recreational cyclists, have immune systems that would put their younger counterparts to shame. It's like our bodies become superheroes, easily fighting off pesky infections and diseases.

Exercise also has a way of slowing down that pesky *"biological clock."*

You know, the one that likes to tick away and remind us of our age?

Researchers have discovered that adults who run, jog, or do any other form of moderate exercise for at least 30-40 minutes five days a week can gain a nine-year "biological aging advantage." It's like we're defying time itself.

How amazing is that?

And let's not forget about our brains.

Well, exercise is like a magic potion for our brains. It improves our mood, boosts our energy, and even enhances our memory and attention span. In fact, studies have shown that moderate to intense exercise can slow down brain aging by a whopping ten years!

So, next time you feel forgetful, just hit the yoga mat or go for a brisk walk. Your brain will thank you.

Now, I know what you're thinking. How do we enjoy all these amazing benefits of exercise?

The good news is that it's never too late to start. Whether you're a lifelong fitness enthusiast or just dipping your toes into the exercise pool, you can reap the rewards. And you don't need to run marathons or spend hours at the gym to see the anti-aging magic happen.

Nope, even a few minutes of daily activity can make a world of difference.

Yoga is like a targeted anti-aging workout that strengthens and tones our bodies, making us feel like superheroes. And it's not just about the physical benefits. Yoga also improves our mobility, reduces the risk of falls, protects our cognitive function, and boosts our mental well-being. It's like a one-stop shop for all things fantastic.

Here are a few of my favorite yoga poses that will have you feeling like a guru in no time:

Side Crow

This pose strengthens your arms and is perfect for unleashing your inner superhero. Squat down, twist your knees to the right, place your hands on the floor, and lift your legs, balancing them on your upper right arm. Repeat on the other side and feel the power!

Goddess Squat

This pose works wonders for your outer thighs. Stand with your feet apart, toes turned out, and squat down as low as you can. Keep your hands praying in front of your chest and feel the burn.

Chair Pose

Get ready to strengthen those glutes! Stand with your feet together, inhale, and lift your arms overhead. Then, exhale and bend your knees, bringing your thighs closer to the floor. Keep your back long and your chest lifted. Rise back up and repeat. You'll feel like you can conquer the world!

Incline Plank

This pose targets the backs of your thighs. Sit on the floor with your legs extended, palms down behind you, and lift your hips, forming a straight line from head to heels. To make it more challenging, lift one leg and point your toes. Who needs a thigh master when you've got yoga?

Chaturanga

Time to strengthen those chest muscles! Begin in a straight-arm plank and slowly lower your body until you hover a few inches off the floor. Push back up to the plank position and feel the burn in all the right places.

Remember, my fellow retirees, the key is to find what works for you and make it a part of your daily routine. Whether it's yoga, walking, dancing, or anything else that gets your heart pumping and your body moving, just keep at it. The benefits are truly endless.

So, let's show the world that aging is just a number, and we're here to rewrite the script. If anyone tells you that aches, pains, and loss of function are acceptable for aging, just smile, nod, and show them your yoga moves. They'll quickly realize we're rewriting aging rules, one pose at a time!

You can't cultivate a growth mindset without intentionally seeking positive inspiration.

You may think, *"Why should I bother with all this mindset stuff? I'm already retired and living the good life!"*

Well, my friends, let me tell you, having a growth mindset is like adding a sprinkle of magic to your golden years.

You see, inspiration is the secret sauce that spices up our lives. It's a spark that ignites our imagination and invigorates us to create, solve problems, and chase after our wildest dreams.

Remember when a brilliant idea seemed to pop out of thin air?

That's inspiration at work. But if you've noticed that your creative mojo isn't flowing as freely as it used to, don't fret. It happens to the best of us, even the most accomplished individuals.

The good news is that your inspiration isn't gone forever; it just needs a little nudge to make a grand entrance again.

So, let's talk about what inspiration is all about. It's like a breath of fresh air, the mental stimulation that fuels our creative fire and brings our dreams to life. It's the zest we need to tackle complex problems, embark on exciting new ventures, and even shake things up to take a different path in life. Inspiration is all about positive thinking, embracing possibilities, and letting our spontaneous thoughts take flight.

Inspiration isn't just a fleeting feeling; it's also tightly intertwined with our mental well-being. When we find ourselves inspired, a surge of motivation and excitement courses through our veins.

And guess what?

That newfound energy brings along some amazing perks. Think improved clarity, boosted energy levels, and a whole lot more creativity.

If you're feeling persistently uninspired and stuck in a slump of self-doubt and frustration, it might be time to pause and assess the situation. Sometimes, those feelings can be a sign of a low mood or even a symptom of depression. And trust me, my friends, there's no shame in seeking help from a mental health professional if you've been feeling down in the dumps for more than a couple of weeks. They're there to lend a hand and guide you to the path of inspiration and joy.

Now, let's get practical and talk about how we can intentionally seek inspiration. It's not about chasing after it with a butterfly net but rather creating the right environment for it to find you.

Remember those times when inspiration struck like lightning, catching you off guard?

Those were the moments when you allowed your thoughts to roam freely without consciously trying to summon inspiration.

So, let's explore some strategies to invite inspiration back into our lives:

Shake Things Up

Break free from the mundane routine and explore new places. Take a trip to an art museum, soak in the beauty, and let those creative ideas flow. And who knows, maybe a masterpiece of your own is just waiting to be born!

Get Your Thoughts On Paper

Set your ideas free by journaling. Don't hold back; let your thoughts flow without worrying about the challenges or the "how" of it all.

Embrace Nature's Embrace

Step outside and let nature work its magic on you. Take a stroll through a park or lose yourself in a community garden. Creativity can bloom like a vibrant spring flower when you let go of those intrusive thoughts and worries.

Reconnect With Your True Self

What lights up your soul? Are there activities you used to be passionate about but somehow lost touch with? Take some time to rediscover those inspirations from yesteryear. It's like rekindling an old flame and finding it burns brighter than ever.

Boost That Self-Esteem

If you're feeling down or plagued by self-doubt, it's time to give your self-worth a little boost. Overcome that impostor syndrome and let your creative spirit soar.

As Vincent Van Gogh once said,

"If you hear a voice within you say, 'you cannot paint,' then by all means, paint!"

Face Your Fears

Fear has a way of cramping our creative style. But what if we pushed fear aside and let our ideas flow without judgment? Imagine the possibilities! As George Addair wisely noted, "*Everything you've ever wanted is on the other side of fear.*"

Surround Yourself With Inspiration

Inspiration is contagious, my friends. So, seek out the company of those riding the wave of creativity. Join online communities or local groups with like-minded individuals who share your interests. And don't forget to keep your distance from those negativity magnets who love to rain on your creative parade.

Don't Pressure Yourself To Be Inspired

Inspiration is a free spirit; it comes and goes as it pleases. So, take a deep breath, acknowledge that you're in an uninspired moment, and give yourself time for those brilliant thoughts to reappear naturally. And hey, in the meantime, why not focus on some practical tasks that need your attention?

Inspiration will make a grand entrance when the time is right.

Here, I must reference Elizabeth Gilbert's captivating book, Big Magic.

She talks about persistence and her own journey as a writer. Boy, did she have to put in some serious effort before her art caught the spotlight!

Remember, we are all art-makers who create a beautiful life. So, take it from Gilbert when she says, "*You must keep trying. You must search tirelessly and faithfully, hoping against hope to someday experience that divine collision of creative communication.*"

Remember, when it all comes together, it's like a gift from the heavens. It's that moment when you can't help but bow down in gratitude as if you've been granted an audience with the divine.

Every one of us has the power to tap into that creative magic.

No magical template can predict what will capture someone's imagination or when that spark will ignite. But what we can do is maximize our chances by playing the odds.

Put yourself out there with stubborn good cheer, and then do it again and again and again. Persistence is the name of the game.

And be sure that the effort is worth it. When you finally make that connection, it's like a symphony of joy and fulfillment.

Creative life isn't always a smooth ride. You try and try, and sometimes it feels like nothing works. But you keep going, my friends. You keep seeking because sometimes everything falls into place when you least expect it. It's like calling out at night for a wild animal on the prowl, and suddenly, you hear the thunder of hooves. And before you know it, that beautiful beast comes rushing into the glade, searching for you as urgently as you've been searching for it.

Let's recap our adventure, shall we?

Feeling uninspired is just a temporary detour, my friends. We can always reignite that creative flame by shaking things up a bit.

Remember to reconnect with your true self. Dive into activities that light up your soul and rediscover your passions. Boost your self-esteem, banish the doubts, and let your creativity shine.

Pema Chödrön's teachings remind us that we can transform our lives by manifesting the reality we desire, even in the face of financial unpreparedness for retirement.

Also, give the Law of Attraction a shot.

Embrace it like Oprah, and make the most of your golden years. Who knows what amazing adventures and experiences are waiting for you?

Remember, the Law of Attraction is always at work in our lives. The question is, will you ignore it or ride the wave of positivity and manifest your dreams?

The choice is yours, my friends. Choose wisely, and let's make our retirements the best they can be!

Chapter 9: Enjoy The Process

Let me share a little story with you.

Recently, I stumbled upon some fitness leaders coaching a funky new movement that involves squatting, sitting on the floor, and getting creative with our bodies.

As a kid, squatting was as natural as breathing, but over time, my knees became stiffer than an ironing board.

But guess what?

This new movement opened up a whole new world for me!

I've regained my ability to squat with much less knee discomfort, and I'm even working on getting up without using my hands.

Who knew that I'd be mastering ninja-like moves at this stage of life?

The best part is that this newfound growth mindset isn't just about physical stuff. We're still living with that old idea that age is like an arch: born, peak at midlife, and decline into decrepitude.

But that's baloney!

Just look at the legendary Jane Fonda, who's had hip and knee replacements and back surgery. She's got osteoarthritis, but she's not letting that stop her from shining bright like the star she is.

Jane is about staying active, and she's got a fitness video that's the bee's knees (literally). She shows us that age is just a number with light yoga stretches and Pilates. The secret sauce is finding exercises that build flexibility, stability, and ease of movement.

And trust me, these routines are shorter than your morning coffee break!

Memory loss isn't a given. Sure, you might have moments of forgetfulness, but it's all part of the grand journey. And don't let anyone tell you you can't learn new tricks!

You can start anything new at any age. Pick up an instrument, learn a foreign language, or maybe even try knitting tiny hats for your cat(s) – why not?

It's all about finding meaning and joy in life. Now that you've got some extra time do what makes your heart sing. Rekindle old hobbies, find new ones, or volunteer for a cause you're passionate about. Your purpose in life doesn't come with an expiration date.

And connection is everything! Stay social! It's like a secret potion for good health. Don't let loneliness knock on your door, Whether old friends, new friends, or furry friends. Join clubs, take classes, and show the world that your social life is booming like never before.

Don't let anyone tell you you're past your prime. Keep moving, stay active, and keep that brain sharp. There's no off switch for learning, and your mind is like a muscle – the more you use it, the stronger it gets. Try out puzzles, brain games, or even challenge yourself to brush your teeth with your non-dominant hand. Venture into the unknown, and you'll be amazed at how much your brain can grow.

And here's a little secret: laughter goes a long way. Keep your spirit young by finding humor in life's quirks and absurdities. Laughter is a magical potion that keeps us balanced, energetic, and joyful – the ultimate fountain of youth.

Speaking of challenges, let's talk about the big one: fear of the unknown. Fear and anxiety can be powerful forces at any age, but we can minimize their impact by having faith and trust in life and other people.

You might be wondering about the spiritual side of aging.

Well, guess what?

Aging affects our spirit, too, and it's a time to review and reflect on our lives. We may question our purpose, regrets, and hopes for the future. It's a time of deep introspection and growth and an essential part of our journey.

Now, let's address the notion that aging means declining health and disability. Oh, no, no, no! Some diseases become more common as we age, but aging doesn't automatically mean poor health or disability. Nope! We can take charge of our health by staying active, eating well, and getting plenty of sleep.

And you know what?

It's never too late to start. Even if you haven't been the healthiest in the past, you can make positive changes now and reap the benefits.

Now, mobility might not be as glamorous as bungee jumping or riding a rollercoaster, but trust me, it's just as important, if not more. It's the key to maintaining our independence and living life fully.

As we gracefully transition into our golden years, it's only natural that we experience changes in mobility. Our gait and balance may alter, and physical strength may wane.

But there's no need to let these changes slow us down. In fact, maintaining and improving our mobility is conducive to living a vibrant and independent life in our later years.

So, let's explore some fantastic ways to keep our bodies moving and grooving:

Warm-Up and Cool Down

It is essential to warm up those joints and muscles before performing exercise. Simple stretches get our bodies primed and ready for action. By loosening up, we can make the most out of our exercise routine and prevent unnecessary strain and potential injuries. Similarly, cooling down after exercising helps our muscles relax and recover, reducing the chances of stiffness and fatigue.

Walk the Walk

Walking is the unsung hero of low-impact exercises. It keeps us active and grants us the gift of fresh air and mental well-being. If you're feeling a bit wobbly, start by taking short walks around your home before gradually working up to more extended strolls outdoors.

Low Impact Cardio

Who says we can't have a blast while staying active? Low-impact cardio exercises like Zumba, kickboxing, or swimming are perfect for seniors looking to stay fit while having fun. And guess what? Senior centers are the ultimate hotspots for group fitness classes and activities, where you can make friends and stay fabulously fit!

Stretch It Out

As we age, stretching becomes even more crucial for maintaining flexibility and range of motion. It's like giving our muscles a daily dose of love and freedom. Regular stretching releases the tension in our fascia tissues, keeping us feeling limber and agile. Who knew that a simple 10-minute stretch could work such wonders?

Balance and Coordination

We may not be walking a tightrope in a circus, but our balance and coordination are vital for a fall-free life. Lightweight training, yoga, and the ever-enchanting tai chi are our secret weapons to staying steady and graceful. Tai chi's slow and deliberate movements improve our strength, flexibility, and reflexes, making us stand tall like seasoned warriors.

Posture Perfect

Slouching? No way, my friends! Proper posture is our ticket to a mobile and strong body. Maintaining a neutral spine position keeps our necks, backs, and shoulders happy. No more strained muscles or joint damage—just the elegance of sitting tall and proud.

Nourish Your Body

Nutrition is the unsung hero of maintaining mobility. Properly balanced meals fuel our bodies for the adventures ahead. Calcium, vitamins D and K, and magnesium keep our bones and muscles in tip-top shape. And let's not forget those omega-3 fatty acids, fighting off muscle and joint discomfort with ease!

And just like avoiding rainy days, steer clear of too much sugar, red meat, and fried foods that can bring on inflammation.

Now, before diving headfirst into any exercise routine, remember to consult your doctor to ensure it's all good to go. Safety first, my friends! And don't forget to wear comfy shoes and clothes that let you move like a breeze.

Retirement is truly a wonderful time in our lives, and it's all about making the most of it with exciting experiences and self-discovery. There are so many ways to enjoy this golden phase, and it's up to us to choose what brings us joy and fulfillment.

One fantastic way to enrich our retirement journey is through meditation. I know what you might be thinking – meditation might be trendy, but is it really for us retirees?

Well, let me tell you, meditation is a powerful tool that offers countless benefits for both our mental and physical well-being.

When it comes to our mental health, meditation can be a game-changer. It helps combat depression, anxiety, and loneliness, giving us a sense of peace and calm.

It's not just alternative health practices that recognize its power. Traditional doctors are also embracing meditation as part of their treatment plans for various conditions.

For those of us concerned about dementia and Alzheimer's, meditation can be a powerful ally. It helps us feel calmer and reduces the perceived stress that can contribute to cognitive decline. Plus, it even slows down the aging rate of our brains by increasing cortical thickness and grey matter.

How amazing is that?

But that's not all – meditation also works wonders for our physical health. It can help with insomnia, chronic pain, high blood pressure, and other physical ailments.

Why? Because our mind and body are deeply interconnected, and when we take care of our mental health, our physical health thrives, too.

Now, I know that diving into meditation might feel overwhelming. There are different types to explore, and it can be challenging to know where to start.

Let's look at some meditation techniques that are perfect for seniors. We have the body scan meditation, a gentle practice that can be done sitting or lying down. It's fantastic for managing pain and even helps us sleep after a rejuvenating yoga session.

If closing your eyes is tricky, don't worry –meditation with your eyes open is an option too. You can try a walking meditation technique, connecting with nature as you stroll along a safe path or trail. And for those looking to enhance body awareness, tai chi classes at local senior centers are a fantastic option.

I won't lie – mindfulness meditation might feel a bit challenging at first. But guided practices make it easier to get into the flow. There is no need to wrestle with your thoughts –follow the guidance and find your Zen.

And speaking of guided meditation, it's like having a personal meditation guru by your side. They'll lead you through a relaxing journey, reducing stress and anxiety. It's like a mini-vacation for your mind!

Have you ever heard of mantra meditation? It's a magical chant that brings you peace and harmony. Some techniques may require a teacher's guidance, but the benefits are worth it.

And if you're all about the breath, then breath-based meditation is your jam! It's simple and effective, offering benefits like lower blood pressure, reduced stress, and better sleep.

The Perks of Hiking for Seniors

Hiking is like a fountain of youth for us. It has a low impact and is gentle on our joints, helping improve our sense of balance, coordination, and cognitive function.

Hiking is a mood booster! Yes, you heard it right. When we hike, our brains release those happy chemicals called endorphins, making us feel on top of the world.

Secondly, hiking is a sensory delight. As we age, our senses sometimes need a bit of a kick-start. Well, guess what? Hiking does just that! The exercise gets the blood flowing to our brains, sharpening our perception of the world around us.

Health Benefits

Hiking is not just a walk in the park; it's a journey to better health! It's a heart-healthy activity that boosts our cardiovascular health and lung function. Plus, it's an excellent remedy for arthritis and joint pain, as it's a low-impact exercise that won't strain our precious joints.

Before You Embark on Your Hike

First things first, let's plan our route and do some research on the terrain. Knowing what we're getting into is essential, especially if we want to enjoy the journey to the fullest. So, check the weather forecast, and if there's a chance of snow or ice on the trail, call those local authorities to get the latest updates.

Staying Safe on the Trail

Safety is a priority, and we want to make sure you have fun without any worries.

Here are some tips to keep in mind:

1. Pace Yourself

There's no need to rush. Hiking is all about enjoying the journey, not breaking speed records. Take your time and go at your own pace.

2. Stick to the Trail

No wild adventures off the beaten path! Stay on the designated trail to avoid any unnecessary risks.

3. Buddy Up

It's always more fun to hike with a buddy or in a group. Besides, having someone along ensures you've got a helping hand if needed.

4. Dress Smart

Comfort is key! Wear appropriate clothing and quality hiking shoes, and don't forget that wide-brimmed hat for sun protection.

5. Hydrate, Hydrate, Hydrate

Always have plenty of water with you. Staying hydrated is crucial for a safe and enjoyable hike.

6. Bring a Map and Emergency Kit

Be prepared for anything. Bring a map of the trail, a first aid kit, and an emergency whistle – better safe than sorry!

Finding the Perfect Trail: Now that we're all set for a safe and fantastic hiking experience, let's choose the right trail. Start small with shorter, easy trails if you're new to hiking. As you gain confidence and fitness, you can tackle more challenging adventures.

Here are some of my recommendations if you live in or are visiting the United States:

Landscape Arch Trail in Arches National Park, Utah

This easy 2-mile out-and-back trail takes you to the stunning Landscape Arch, a natural wonder worth seeing. The trail is relatively flat and shows the Utah desert's beauty.

Maroon Bells Scenic Loop Trail in Aspen, Colorado

This picturesque 2-mile loop offers breathtaking views of the Maroon Bells, famous for their majestic beauty. The trail is relatively flat, making it accessible for seniors to soak in the splendor of the Colorado mountains.

Dukes Creek Trail in Helen, Georgia

This 2.2-mile out-and-back trail takes you to a beautiful waterfall surrounded by a serene forest. The initial part is paved, leading to an observation deck, making it a stroll.

The Zion Narrows Riverside Walk in Zion National Park, Utah

This paved 1.8-mile trail follows the Virgin River, surrounded by towering canyon walls. It's a perfect way for seniors to experience the beauty of Zion without strenuous hiking.

Torrey Pines Beach Trail Loop in Del Mar, California

This 2.3-mile loop offers spectacular coastal views and easy walking on mostly paved trails. It's a great way to enjoy the ocean breeze and soak in the natural beauty of California's coast.

Hoh Rain Forest's Hall of Moss in Olympic National Park, Washington

This short 1.1-mile trail takes you through an enchanting rainforest adorned with moss and ferns. It's an easy hike, perfect for immersing yourself in nature.

Giant City Nature Trail in Southern Illinois

This 1-mile loop with only a 160-foot elevation gain takes you through a magical forest with unique rock formations. It's a delightful hike for you to explore the beauty of the Shawnee National Forest.

Remember, each of these trails provides a unique and unforgettable experience, and they are all suitable for retirees looking to enjoy the wonders of nature without overexertion.

Retirement Retreats

So, we're in the prime of our lives. We've got all that wisdom, a boldness we've never felt before, and guess what? We're finally free from all those worldly shackles! It's time to take a breath, hit that restart button, and live life the way we always wanted. It's time to reinvent ourselves, try new talents, and embrace our beloved hobbies.

And you know what?

A little getaway might be the perfect thing to spice things up.

Now, some of us have already discovered the wonders of yoga, keeping our bodies vibrant and minds sharp. But hey, if you haven't tried it yet, don't worry. A yoga retreat is just what the doctor ordered.

Imagine soulful yogic techniques, exotic locations, and a chance to let go of all that negativity that's been piling up over the years.

Sounds pretty awesome, right? Well, that's because it is!

Yoga has been around for over 5,000 years; let me tell you, it's the real deal. Not only does it rejuvenate our bodies and help us stay agile, but it also gives us that sense of unity and mindfulness we need in life.

You get to bask in a holistic yogic experience at a yoga retreat. You'll have expert instructors guiding you through the practice, an ambiance as serene as a calm lake, and food as nourishing as homemade soup.

Yoga retreats take you away from that mundane routine and drop you into the lap of nature's beauty. Imagine starting your day with a refreshing yoga class, surrounded by breathtaking landscapes.

As we age, we might face a few challenges – we all know that. Yoga addresses all those challenges. It keeps our muscles flexible, our minds sharp, and our spirits high. And speaking of spirits, yoga has this amazing way of connecting us with ourselves, our emotions, and even with our fellow yoga buddies. Trust me, you'll make some fabulous friends on these retreats. They'll be like-minded people worldwide, ready to explore, learn, and grow just like you.

And the best part?

You're never too old to do yoga! Whether you're a seasoned yogi or a complete newbie doesn't matter. A yoga retreat will make you feel like a true yoga master.

Now, let's talk about fasting retreats. They're quite the trend, too, but you know what? They're not new at all. Fasting has been around for centuries, used by different cultures and religions to grow faith and reconnect with our inner selves.

Fasting retreats can be an incredible way to reflect on life, cleanse your body and mind, and enjoy the benefits of fasting in a safe and supportive setting. It's like hitting the reset button on your whole system!

You'll have professional therapists and medical experts guiding you all the way, ensuring you get the most out of your fasting journey.

And let me tell you, the benefits are pretty mind-blowing. Some of the perks are improved weight loss and management, greater focus and concentration, renewed energy, and a stronger spiritual connection. It's like a journey of self-discovery that leaves you feeling like a whole new person.

Remember, the world is your oyster, and these golden years are for you to enjoy to the fullest!

Chapter 10: Conclusion

My dear friends, can you believe we're at the end of our retirement adventure?

Let me start by saying that we are the fearless few! You see, having a solid plan for our golden years is a bit of a rarity, but that's what makes us special.

So, I sincerely hope that *"Retirement on a Shoestring: Ideas in Support of a Fearless, Creative Final Chapter"* has acted as a guide that has reassured you, inspired you, and nudged you toward embracing this beautiful phase of life.

I'm just an ordinary retiree like you, but as I mentioned at the beginning of this book, I'm no stranger to the "go with the flow" approach. It's taken me on wild adventures and taught me to trust the process without fear. As carefree as I may have been, living in the moment didn't exactly set me up for a financially secure retirement. I hope you learned the lessons that I knew, and they widened your perspective toward your retirement.

Here's a recap of the essence of what you might have learned so far:

Unplanned Retirement Realities

I was living my life to the fullest, chasing after my dreams, and having a grand ol' time. But as the years flew by like birds on a migration spree, reality started knocking on my door, or should I say, my wallet?

You must realize that relying solely on social security isn't the golden ticket to financial freedom. It's more like the fast track to becoming a Walmart greeter or flipping burgers at the nearest fast-food joint.

Finding Financial Independence

We're the masters of adaptation, right?

So, it's time to explore alternative income streams that grant us the freedom we deserve. I researched and gave you valuable ideas for discovering multiple income streams. From renting out an "alternative dwelling unit" to exploring the world of online tutoring or becoming a notary public, there's something for everyone.

The Adventure Begins

Now, I won't lie; getting started can be a bit overwhelming. But I hope my financial advice changed your take on this matter. Scale back that 8-hour job as much as possible and make time for this exciting exploration. Dive into the research, use job search engines, and attend those free seminars on social media. Trust me; you'll find some hidden gems in there!

But be wary, take notes, research, and check those customer/client reviews. You don't want to be left with just an empty wallet and a broken dream.

The Perfect Fit

Remember, this is your retirement adventure, and you've got to find the right fit for you. It's like trying on a pair of shoes – you want them to be comfortable and stylish. So, seek out something that aligns with your unique skills and life experience. Use your creativity to discover new paths, and let your intuition guide you. After all, there are no accidents; every opportunity is a step toward your perfect fit.

Focus, Focus, Focus!

Be fearless explorers! Once you've chosen your path, it's time to buckle down and get to work. Stay laser-focused and resist the temptation to chase every shiny opportunity that comes your way. You've got this, and I know you can make it happen! Don't forget about time management – it's the key to balancing it all.

The Power of Appreciation

Now, let's talk about something magical: the power of appreciation. You'll discover a new sense of purpose and fulfillment when you find your perfect fit. I, for one, found that my work in the non-profit world was not only meaningful but also mentally and emotionally invigorating. And you know what's icing on the cake? Being surrounded by a younger generation keeps me feeling young at heart!

Embrace the Growth Mindset

All right, my health-conscious friends here's where we dive into the self-care domain. I have a long history with this stuff, from owning a health foods store to teaching yoga classes. So, take my advice. Let's meditate, visualize our dreams, and affirm the life we want. And let's not forget to stay physically fit – healthy bodies, healthy minds, right?

Savoring the Journey

Last but not least, let's savor this retirement journey! Age is just a number, and our cognitive, physical, and spiritual selves can thrive at any stage of life.

So, let's enjoy every moment, welcome the challenges with a positive mindset, and revel in discovering new passions and possibilities. This is our time, fearless retirees, and we will make the most of it!

Well, folks, I gotta say, it has been an absolute honor to have you all here, sharing this wild ride we call "retirement" with me.

And let me tell you, it's been a real journey of self-discovery and adventure. Now, I want you to remember that this book is no cookie-cutter solution to retirement. Oh no, it's all about embracing that curiosity, gratitude, and excitement and using them to whip up your perfect recipe for this chapter of your life.

You see, life's full of surprises; believe me, I've had my fair share. Just as I was navigating the twists and turns of retirement, life threw me a curveball. I was there, standing strong as the primary caregiver for my sweet mother, and then she left us. It was devastating and emotional. Moments like these make you stop and think about what truly matters in life.

But hey, amidst the ups and downs, I've seen my teenage grandkids growing up, finding their wings, and soaring to new heights. And let me tell you, it isn't always easy to keep up with those young ones! But I'm determined to stay close to them and be that cool grandparent with all the wisdom to share.

Sometimes, life has a funny way of making us practice what we preach. And for me, that means staying on the sunny side of gratitude. Even in the most challenging moments, I've found a glimmer of hope and joy. And my hope, dear friends, is that something I've shared in this book will give you that extra boost to tackle this final chapter of life with a big ol' smile.

So, my fellow retirees, let's embrace this new phase with open arms and hearts. It's a time for growth, a time for taking care of ourselves, and a time for finding that fresh sense of purpose. Together, we can paint this chapter with vibrant colors of health, happiness, and a renewed zest for life.

Life's too short to be stuck in the same old routine. No, sir, it's time to dust off those dreams, blow off the cobwebs of doubt, and fearlessly step into this beautiful unknown. Retirement is certainly not the end of the road; it's the beginning of a grand adventure.

Let's face this final chapter with courage, creativity, and a sprinkle of humor. Together, we'll show the world that retirement is not a downhill ride but a thrilling voyage filled with endless opportunities.

So, let's ride this retirement wave with laughter, joy, and the spirit of endless possibilities. I'm cheering you on every step of the way, my friends!

Get out there, and let's make this the best chapter yet! Cheers to a fearless and creative retirement!

References

1. Achebe, C. (n.d.). Things Fall Apart [Review of the book Things Fall Apart]. Briefer.

2. Benton, C. (2020, January 9). Stay Productive in Retirement. Scribbling Boomer. https://www.scribblingboomer.com/stay-productive-in-retirement/

3. Beres, D. (2017, May 18). 3 techniques for overcoming anxiety. Big Think. https://bigthink.com/mind-brain/3-techniques-for-overcoming-anxiety

4. Bliss, S. (2019, April 29). 9 Ways To Find Your Perfect Career Match. Forbes. https://www.forbes.com/sites/sarabliss/2019/04/29/9-ways-to-find-your-perfect-career-match/?sh=2f202a1cec75

5. CEO Today Magazine. (2022, March 8). How to Find the Right Job That Matches Your Skills. https://www.ceotodaymagazine.com/2022/03/how-to-find-the-right-job-that-matches-your-skills/

6. Collamer, N. (2018, July 31). How to Find a Great Part-Time Job in Retirement. Forbes. https://www.forbes.com/sites/nextavenue/2018/07/31/how-to-find-a-great-part-time-job-in-retirement/?sh=26c0383622e5

7. Evans, J. (2018, July 19). Pema Chodron's Places That Scare You: A Guide to Fearlessness in Difficult Times [Review of the book Places That Scare You: A Guide to Fearlessness in Difficult Times, by Pema Chodron]. Philosophy for Life. https://www.philosophyforlife.org/blog/pema-chodrons-places-that-scare-you

8. Fekri, S. (2022, April 16). Time Management in Retirement and Why Is It Crucial? Living Maples. https://livingmaples.com/mag/time-management-in-retirement-and-why-is-it-crucial/

9. Fisher, A. (n.d.). Using Intuition in Your Job Search: Hot Jobs. Monster.com. Monster Career Advice https://www.monster.com/career-advice/article/using-intuition-in-your-job-search-hot-jobs

10. Hagen, S. (2019, January 9). Create Coaching & Consulting. How to Use Your Intuition in Business https://www.createcoachingconsulting.com/how-to-use-your-intuition-in-business/

11. Harvard Health Publishing. (2014, March 9). Exercise and aging: Can you walk away from Father Time? https://www.health.harvard.edu/staying-healthy/exercise-and-aging-can-you-walk-away-from-father-time.

https://briefer.com/books/things-fall-apart

12. Hurst, K. (n.d.). Oprah Winfrey on the Law of Attraction. The Law of Attraction. https://thelawofattraction.com/oprah-winfrey-on-the-law-of-attraction

13. Lee, T. (2014, May 29). Let Your Intuition Be Your Guide. CareerCast. https://www.careercast.com/career-news/let-your-intuition-be-your-guide

14. Leung, A. (2022, February 26). How Many Side Hustles Is Too Many? Medium. https://andrewleung14.medium.com/how-many-side-hustles-is-too-many-54a7608eb4b0

15. National Council on Aging. (2022, October 11). How exercise helps you age well. https://ncoa.org/article/how-exercise-helps-you-age-well

16. Schaffer, A. (2017, January 11). Yoga Workout for Anti-Aging. Health. https://www.health.com/fitness/yoga-workout-anti-aging

17. Seegert, L. (2021, June 1). How Exercise Fights Aging. Time. https://time.com/6053055/how-exercise-fights-aging

18. Sightings, T. (2018, June 15). 10 Tips for Managing Time in Retirement. U.S. News & World Report. https://money.usnews.com/money/blogs/on-retirement/articles/2018-06-15/10-tips-for-managing-time-in-retirement

19. Tepper, T., & Curry, B. (2022, April 13). 3 Lessons For Helping Retirees Get Back To Work. Forbes Advisor. https://www.forbes.com/advisor/retirement/how-to-work-in-retirement/

20. Wild, J. (n.d.). Retiring Not Shy. Planning for Retirement: Time Management in Retirement - Get the Most out of Life https://retiringnotshy.com.au/planning/time-management-in-retirement-get-the-most-out-of-life/

Made in the USA
Monee, IL
11 November 2026

f20f24cc-e5db-4161-b656-c2f4e4fd8f0eR01